Only
Correct

Only Correct

The Best of Corrections & Clarifications

Ian Mayes

Guardian Books

First published in 2005 by Guardian Books

Copyright © 2005 The Guardian
Guardian Books is an imprint of Guardian Newspapers Ltd.

The right of Ian Mayes to be identified as author of this work
has been asserted by him in accordance with section 77 of the
Copyright, Designs and Patents Act, 1988.

The Guardian and MediaGuardian are trademarks
of the Guardian Media Group plc and Guardian Newspapers Ltd.

A CIP record for this book is available from the British Library upon request

ISBN: 1 84354 465 2

Distributed by Atlantic Books
An imprint of Grove Atlantic Ltd., Ormond House,
26-27 Boswell Street, London WC1N 3JZ

Cover Design: Two Associates
Text Design: www.carrstudio.co.uk

Printed in Great Britain by Cambridge University Press

10 9 8 7 6 5 4 3 2 1

To my colleagues scattered too thinly round the world in the
Organisation of News Ombudsmen, the aptly acronymed
ONO

Ian Mayes has donated his fee for this book
to the embryonic Hazlitt Society

Acknowledgments

Quite apart from the journalists and readers of the Guardian, I have to acknowledge a large number of people, starting with the editor of the Guardian, Alan Rusbridger. I am, so to speak, his brainchild, instantly weaned with a contract under which he and the owners of the Guardian, the Scott Trust, guarantee my independence — exercising that independence is the principal way I have of thanking them for it. I particularly want to say a warm thank you to my two main props, the assistant readers' editor Helen Hodgson, and my colleague and most frequent deputy Murray Armstrong. Leslie Plommer, Barbara Harper, John Cunningham and Nikki Marshall, have all stood in for me for spells in the period covered by this book. I have been very fortunate in the succession of helpers I have had from day one, among them, Kate McLaughlin, Rose de Paeztron and Caroline Furneaux, who in addition has helped me put together all three of these books of corrections. Chris Elliott, the managing editor of the Guardian, who deals with complaints that escape me and go to the Press Complaints Commission, has not let this spoil our friendship. His assistant, Wendy Collinson, and the other members of the editor's support staff, have been wonderfully helpful when needed — I should mention Doreen Pallier, Jo Wood, Rosie Bower, and Martyn Dore. Finally my thanks to the publisher at the Guardian, Lisa Darnell.

Introduction

'It's only human nature that a chap should go on making mistakes until he dies'
– Svejk in *The Good Soldier Svejk*, Jaroslav Hasek trs Cecil Parrott.

The corrections in this book represent the essential lighter side of my job as readers' editor of the Guardian, a role in which I referee complaints about the paper's journalism. It is sometimes a rough game. Perhaps this is the place, however, to emphasise that, viewed in the round, and bearing in mind the prodigious quantity of stuff produced by the Guardian, there is very little wrong with its journalism, and even less with its journalists. If I had to sum up their attitude towards me over the past years of exposing to the world their lapses, excesses and occasional aberrations (and some of my own in the process), the word to spring to mind would be supportive. Everything considered, I have worked in an amazingly tantrum-free environment. A tear comes to my eye as I thank them for that. Without them, don't let us forget, this book would not have been possible. By the way, putting the corrections in categories for the first time, for example, arts, science, sport, does not imply relative judgments of one department against another. The titles are simply those of rough classes of mistake gathered from the four corners of the Guardian and do not, invidiously, indicate a hierarchy of error or the level of sin in a particular department.

The corrections here, I emphasise, exclude all the more serious ones for which the daily column in the newspaper primarily exists, and publishing them does not imply any lack of sincerity or commitment to the main task. They are drawn from the whole period of my activity as readers' editor since I became, in November 1997, the first person in the United Kingdom — in the history of British journalism, in fact — to hold such an independent role. This book therefore includes a good many corrections that were published in its two predecessors, *Corrections & Clarifications, 2000*, and *More Corrections & Clarifications, 2002*. They seemed worth keeping in circulation with the substantial number of those that have followed in the past three years. Incidentally, if a faint whiff of erudition comes off any of these corrections I hasten to say it is nothing to do with me and emanates almost entirely from readers of the Guardian.

The previous two books contained a substantial number of my weekly columns dealing with ethical issues and other serious matters. This book contains just a few columns and, with one exception, only those responding to readers' interest in, and sometimes disbelief at, the Guardian's use of the English language. I hope my passion for dictionaries comes across in these. I owe them a great deal. The Guardian default dictionary, the one which journalists are advised to consult in the absence of guidance in the Guardian stylebook, is the admirable *Collins*. I also enjoy using, among relative newcomers, the *Bloomsbury English Dictionary* whose definitions are often wonderfully succinct. But no experience can match that of diving into the huge *Oxford English Dictionary* and bathing in the marvellous language on the surface of which we often splash around so ineffectually — as you will see in the following pages. The exception I mentioned — and the only one of these columns published in the previous books — is a column dealing with the Guardian's frustrated struggles with languages other than English. The embarrassments recorded in this include that of presenting as the Finnish author of an article a name that turned out to mean "Continued on the next page". But I don't want to spoil it for you. Remember as you read on, none of us is perfect.

Ian Mayes
February 2005

correction *n* 1 the act or process of correcting. 2 something offered or substituted for an error; an improvement. 3 the act or process of punishing; reproof. 4 a number or quantity added to or subtracted from a scientific or mathematical calculation or observation to increase its accuracy.

(Collins)

ARTS

29 Apr 1998

In the obituary of Joan Heal, page 13, April 27, we referred to the show "which turned her into a star" as *Grab Me a Gondolier*. Not quite. It should have read *Grab Me a Gondola*.

15 Oct 1998

The unmissable concert by the Philharmonia, which we reviewed on page 15, G2, yesterday, was at the Royal Festival Hall and not at the Royal Albert Hall.

11 Jan 1999

Programme note for Artist of the Week, Radio 3, January 8, told readers that Joan Bakewell would be talking to the German soprano, Dietrich Fischer-Dieskau. Fischer-Dieskau, the German baritone, enjoys a reputation as – to quote Alan Blyth in *The New Grove Dictionary of Music and Musicians* – one of the leading singers of his time, an artist distinguished by his full, resonant voice. Apologies.

17 Jul 1999

In our review of *Last Dance at Dum Dum* (a play at the New Ambassadors, London), page 25, July 15, we said Dum Dum was an old colonial bungalow. In fact, it is a suburb of Calcutta.

2 Nov 1999

In wishing the actor Juliet Stevenson happy 43rd birthday on Saturday, page 24, October 30, we listed among her hits *The Duchess of Mali*. This was inadvertent discrimination against John Webster's *Duchess of Malfi*.

16 Nov 1999

The bugle in the picture on page 9, November 12, was a cornet.

9 Dec 1999

The film starring Errol Flynn in which Gillian Lynne appeared, page 16, G2, December 7, was *The Master of Ballantrae*, not *The Mask of Gallantry*.

● **25 Jan 2000**

In the Guide, page 33, January 22, we remarked how tough it must have been for Gwen John "growing up in the shadow of her father, the illustrious but rather overrated painter Augustus John". She had no such problem. Augustus John (1878-1961) was not her father, he was her younger brother. (Gwen John: 1876-1939).

● **28 Apr 2000**

The Idlewild album reviewed on April 21, page 16, G2 is called *100 Broken Windows*, not *200 Broken Mirrors*.

● **20 Jun 2000**

Diana Ross, the children's writer and illustrator, Obituaries, page 20, yesterday, was a consultant in the development of the children's TV series *Camberwick Green*, not *Candlewick Green* (candlewick perhaps belongs to the same cosy world: it is a material associated with dressing gowns and bedspreads).

● **14 Sep 2000**

The play at the Almeida in London is *Conversations After a Burial*, as our review, page 18, yesterday, indicated, and not *Conversations After a Funeral* as a caption to the accompanying picture said (even though it may amount to the same thing).

● **10 Oct 2000**

Margaret Rutherford was not an "unforgettable Lady Bracknell" (the Guide, page 19, October 7) in Anthony Asquith's film of *The Importance of Being Earnest* (1952). That was Edith Evans. Margaret Rutherford was unforgettable as Miss Prism.

● **13 Feb 2001**

In our piece about the exhibition of Italian paintings of the 18th century, Settecento: Tiepolo's Century, at Lille, page 11, G2, yesterday, we mentioned Guardi's *Emmaus's Supper* and went on to speak of the painting as though Emmaus were the name of a man rather than a village "outside Jerusalem" (Luke, ch 24, verses 13-35). Paintings of the subject are usually called *The Supper at Emmaus*. The famous Venetian church Santa Maria della Salute is usually referred to by that name in French as it is, also, in English.

● **22 Oct 2001**

In a caption to a picture accompanying a report of the appointment of a new artistic director for the Bayreuth Festival we said he might raise a few eyebrows "as well as arias". There are no arias in Wagner's *Ring*.

11 Dec 2001

The former director of the National Theatre is Richard Eyre, not Eyres (Northern light heads south, page 11, December 7). In the same piece we mentioned a JB Priestley play, *Johnson over Johnson*. The correct title is *Johnson over Jordan*.

21 Aug 2002

The surrealist artist Rene Magritte popped up unexpectedly in our third leader, Late at the Tate, page 17, yesterday. When we said "[Picasso] used Magritte's gift, a portrait of his daughter, Marguerite ..." we meant to say "Matisse's gift".

18 Sep 2002

The author of *Oroonoko*, radio review, page 20, G2, September 16, was Aphra Behn, not Benn.

1 Oct 2002

In Web watch, page 6, Online, September 26, we said of JS Bach's the Art of Fugue, "Some believe it contains a coded last will and testament, while others argue the work is unfinished". In fact, it is generally accepted that they have won the argument.

29 Nov 2002

It is Birnam Wood in *Macbeth*, not Burnham (a column, In the hands of the three witches, page 22, November 27).

Burnham Beeches is a wood in Buckinghamshire, unconnected with *Macbeth*.

2 Dec 2002

We should have made it clear in correcting the spelling of Birnam Wood (this column, November 29), that the author of the piece spelt it correctly in his reference to *Macbeth*, and we changed it.

6 Dec 2002

The play scheduled for the spring season at Stratford, page 9, yesterday, is *The Taming of the Shrew*, rather than *The Taming of the Screw*.

21 Feb 2003

In a review, page 20, February 17, we said that Haydn's trumpet concerto was "among the first works written for a valved brass instrument". In fact it was written for a keyed trumpet. The valved trumpet did not come in until the 19th century.

2 Dec 2003

In a column, page 7, Weekend, April 19, we said that an on-stage mishap involving Maria Callas during a performance of *La Sonnambula* at Edinburgh (in 1957) caused laughter, implying that, as a result, she "left Edinburgh the next day, never to return". Whatever the audience reaction to the mishap, it had nothing to do with the reasons for her departure. She left because she had fulfilled her contractual obligations.

12 Jan 2004
In Portrait of the Week, page 17, Review, January 10, we referred to the painting by Lucas Cranach the Elder, *Venus Complaining to Cupid*. That should be *Cupid Complaining to Venus*.

19 Jan 2004
The "dog" hanging from a tree in Andrew Wyeth's painting *Tenant Farmer*, page 14, G2, January 15, is a deer.

22 Jan 2004
The PG Woosterish high jinks, mentioned in a column headed At the risk of sounding like a potty lifestyle guru, etc (page 5, Education, January 20), should, strictly speaking, be PG Wodehouse-ish high jinks.

12 May 2004
In an article, The English disease, page 8, Friday Review, May 7, we misquoted the lyrics of the Bob Dylan song Summer Days. It is not "I'm standing on the table proposing a toast to decay". It is "I'm standing on the table proposing a toast to the King," referring to Elvis Presley.

24 May 2004
In an article, It's not haute cuisine, page 14, G2, May 20, we referred to "the composer Georg Solti". Conductor, in fact.

7 Jul 2004
In our front-page report of the death of Marlon Brando, July 3, we said that Brando sent Sacheen Littlefeather to accept an Oscar for *The Godfather* on his behalf. He sent her to reject it, not to accept it.

24 Aug 2004
The reference to "Brussels' many beautiful turn-of-the-century art deco houses" in Mandelson bonds in Brussels, page 2, August 21, was misplaced. We should have said art nouveau not art deco, which came much later.

6 Sep 2004
Tamara de Lempicka's paintings encapsulated art deco and not, as we said in Pick of the week, art nouveau (G2, page 18, August 30).

26 Jan 2005
The music of the Internationale was composed by Pierre Degeyter, not Degaytre as it appeared in Corrections, page 29, January 21.

BOOKS

24 Aug 1998

In a report on the Finance and Economics page, page 21, August 21, we referred to the £250,000 advance for Vikram Seth's prize-winning novel, *A Suitable Buy*. Although undoubtedly worth every penny, the book is actually called *A Suitable Boy*.

8 Sep 1998

In our report about the comic strip version of *A la recherche du temps perdu* (page 12, yesterday), we added 10 years to Proust's age. He was born on July 10, 1871, and died on November 18, 1922, making him 51 not 61.

6 May 1999

In an article about Thom Gunn on the books pages of the Saturday Review, page 10, May 1, we referred to "the obtuse Elizabethan poet, Fulke Greville". The writer of the piece meant to say abstruse, not obtuse.

1 Jul 2000

Blind Pew was the bearer of the black spot in *Treasure Island*, not Blind Pugh.

3 Aug 2000

In All Abroad, an article about holiday destinations, G2, page 2, yesterday, we misidentified Laurence Durrell as author of *My Family and Other Animals*. It was, of course, written by his brother Gerald. In any case Lawrence Durrell spelt his name with a w.

7 Oct 1998

Nietzsche was misspelt twice in yesterday's Country Diary, page 22.

1:30 Lunch with Niets Neetz Nietzsch Emma

28 Nov 2000

In an article on the paperbacks page of the Saturday Review, page 11, November 25, we twice mentioned the new book by Terry Jones and on both occasions got it wrong. We called it *The Knight and His Lady*, and *The Squire and His Lady*. It is, in fact, called *The Lady and the Squire*. The page heading notwithstanding, it is a hardback.

● **20 Jan 2001**

The details of Derek Malcolm's new book, page 5, G2, January 18, were correct except for the title, publisher and price. The book is *A Century of Films: Derek Malcolm's Personal Best* (not *Derek Malcolm's Personal Best: A Century of Films*). The publisher's name is IB Tauris (not ID Tauris), but more specifically the imprint is Tauris Parke Paperbacks. The price is £9.99 not £9.95.

● **6 Feb 2001**

In a review of a book about Palestine under the British mandate, Books, page 8, Saturday Review, February 3, we made CP Snow the editor of the Manchester Guardian, allowing him, embarrassingly, to usurp the position of the Guardian's most famous editor, CP Scott. The writer of the review was, as we said, Colin Shindler, the author of *Israel, Likud and the Zionist Dream*, not to be confused with Colin Shindler, the author of *Manchester United Ruined My Life*, who also writes for the Guardian. The Guardian itself must take all the responsibility for allowing this particular mistake to reach the printed page.

● **16 Mar 2002**

It is Sir John Nott, the former defence secretary, who has just published his memoirs – *Here Today, Gone Tomorrow*. It is Nott not Knott, as it incorrectly appeared in yesterday's Diary, page 22.

● **7 Feb 2001**

"Mary Shelley's *Dracula*", mentioned in a column, page 5, G2, yesterday, is, of course, Bram Stoker's. Mary Shelley wrote *Frankenstein*.

● **26 Feb 2002**

It was not Queen Victoria who said "My Lord, I had forgot the fart," as we seemed to imply, Weekend, page 24, February 23. It was Queen Elizabeth I to Edward de Vere, Earl of Oxford (1550-1604) on his return to court after seven years of self-imposed exile after breaking wind in the royal presence (John Aubrey, *Brief Lives*).

● **27 Feb 2002**

In our look at the Laugharne of Dylan Thomas, page 12, Travel, February 23, we had Molly Garter among the characters of *Under Milk Wood*. We meant Polly Garter (perhaps we were thinking of Molly Bloom).

● **5 Jul 2002**

Whatever the characteristics of *Howards End*, it does not have an apostrophe (Television, page 22, G2, yesterday).

● **10 Sep 2002**

In our review of the audio version of *Vasari's Lives*, page 28, Review, September 7, we said it was Piero della Francesca's appetite for hardboiled eggs to which he referred. In fact, the egg eater was Piero di Cosimo.

● **1 Oct 2002**

A retrospective correction: In our archive review of *The Magic Mountain* from the Manchester Guardian of July 1, 1927 (page 7, Review, September 7) we referred twice to the excellent translation by Mr Lowe-Porter. H[elen] T[racy] Lowe-Porter (1876-1963) was a woman.

● **5 Nov 2002**

Illustrator and author Tove Jansson is a woman and not, as we said, "the man who wrote and illustrated the wonderful Moomintroll books" (the Editor, page 10, November 2).

● **23 Apr 2003**

In Books in the media, page 39, Review, April 19, we referred to the film of James McCann's novel *Double Indemnity*. We meant to say James M Cain.

● **16 May 2003**

The scene in *The Leopard* in which Angelica (Claudia Cardinale) disgraces herself with raucous laughter takes place at Donnafugata and not at the Duke's palace in Palermo, page 10, G2, May 9.

● **29 Jan 2004**

Candidate for the most persistent error: TS Eliot wrote *The Waste Land*, not *The Wasteland* (Keepers of the flame, page 17, January 24).

● **13 May 2004**

A rogue apostrophe crept into *Finnegans Wake* (That old Greenspan magic seems to be fading, page 23, May 10).

● **26 Jan 2005**

The arch enemy of William Brown was Hubert Lane, not Violet Elizabeth Bott (Q1, The quiz, page 76, Weekend, January 22).

OPEN DOOR
Pardon my accent:

The Readers' Editor on... attempts to cross the language barrier

Alle Menschen werden Brüder – a reasonable sentiment, you might think, for a liberal newspaper to profess, but it would almost certainly be better if we skipped the German of Schiller's *An die Freude* and expressed our joy, even roughly, in English as, say, "We are all in this together".

We like to use foreign words, terms, phrases, but we often get them wrong. We even trip on common names, such as Giuseppe who regularly becomes Guiseppe – Gwee-seppy.

Not long ago, to illustrate a point, we introduced a purely fictional Venezuelan maid into a story and called her Consuela. This brought a sharp note from a woman called, like thousands of other women in the Spanish-speaking world, Consuelo.

"I really have had enough of show-off ignoramuses messing up my name. Consuelo is a Spanish abstract noun, masculine, invariable. Pilar and Mercedes are also Spanish female names derived, like Consuelo, from titles of the Virgin Mary." It would be equally silly, she said, to stick an "a" on them.

Names requiring accents seem to pose even greater difficulties. Extreme, and one has to say transparent, efforts are sometimes made to ensure that accents appear in the correct position. Alas, these efforts sometimes fail. They have caused us to refer to the soprano Christine Schäfer as Christine Schumlautafer, and a work by Liszt became Funacuteerailles. The latter prompted a witty but wounding one-word rejoinder from a reader, "Imbacuteeciles!"

Accent-induced anxiety is common among British journalists who find it difficult to understand why anyone should bother with such things. Foreign words that come into the English language bearing accents are stripped of them when the opportunity arises. Thus when I devoted a recent column to the cliché, you would have found when you picked the paper up on Saturday that I had been writing about the cliche, a deprivation, let us concede, more acute than grave. The tendency that it represents, although it may be seen by some as betraying our accents, is perhaps a good one. It is intended not as a slight – an act or omission indicating supercilious neglect or indifference (*Collins*) – aimed at a word's foreign origins, so much as an embrace or friendly adoption.

Paradoxically, the same anxiety I have mentioned often leads us to use accents like a condiment and to pepper foreign words with them more or less at random, so that readers who know about these things – a large, cosmopolitan and long-suffering congregation – have to ask us to desist. Here are just a couple of examples: The French word for a cluster of racing cyclists is peloton, not péléton (It has nothing to do with a famous Brazilian footballer, this reader added, rather unnecessarily). Congratulations on getting Länder right, another wrote, but the singular is Land not Länd ... and so on.

A recent article on menu French was returned marked in red ink by a reader with an indigestible total of more than 30 errors, most of them relating to missing or misplaced accents.

We get worse as we move farther from Britain. We sometimes manage the diacritical tilde on Spanish words – mañana, for example – and sometimes not. For instance, a native or inhabitant of Madrid is a madrileño/a, not a madrileno.

During the World Cup coverage of 1998 a reader wrote to inquire why, since the Germans generally carried their umlauts proudly on to the pitch, and the French sometimes sported their accents, players of almost all other nationalities left theirs in the dressing room. Møller was always Moller, the Argentine Verón and the Colombian Rincón stepped similarly naked on to the field.

The Czech composers Janácek and Dvorák may get their acute accents but the chances of parading the caron, the little v carried above the c and the r respectively, in the pages of the Guardian are practically nil because of technical difficulties. Their appearance as Janáček and Dvořák is not only rare, it is, at present, almost impossible.

If you are Finnish, then, well, I am tempted to say forget it. We once misspelt the Finnish word for dyslexia (lukihäiriö). A few years ago we carried an article in translation from the Finnish daily newspaper Helsingin Sanomat. The article was fine but the byline turned out to be not the name of the author but the Finnish for "Continued on the next page".

Does any of this really matter? I think it does. I tend to agree with those readers who see it as a kind of parochialism detracting from their view of the Guardian as a paper with an unlimited horizon. Our style guide advises us only to keep all accents on French words and umlauts in German.* Beyond that we are on our own. Neglecting to get it right may be due to carelessness. It can look like prejudice.

15 Jan 2000

* Spanish has now had its accents restored

NAMES

Names

● **12 Nov 1997**

An item headed Slow reader, on the front of our Society section, July 15, referred to a man who returned to a library in Manchester a copy of *Kidnapped* by Robert Louis Stephenson, after keeping it for 65 years. The author, as a descendant of his wrote to remind us, spelt his name with a V not PH: as in R L Stevenson.

● **2 Oct 1998**

In an article on page 2, Friday Review, September 25, we referred to Mamie Eisenhower, the wife of the former US president, as Marnie.

● **3 Nov 1998**

Among our tributes to Ted Hughes, page 5, October 30, there was one which inadvertently suggested he demanded to be read alongside Rupert Graves. Rupert Graves is an actor; Robert Graves was the poet.

● **28 Mar 2000**

The women's acappella group to which we intended to refer on page 13 of the Guide (North edition), March 25, under Liverpool-Merseyside Festival, is Soul Purpose, not Foul Purpose.

● **10 Jan 2001**

The Colombian officer overseeing the police operation described on pages 8 and 9, G2, January 8, was Colonel Bonilla, rather than Colonial Bonilla.

● **6 Apr 2001**

The husband of the Countess of Wessex, page 1, yesterday, is not the Count of Wessex. He is the Earl of Wessex.

● **28 Jul 2001**

Lady Macbeth of Mtsensk, having appeared in the Guardian as *Lady Macbeth of Minsk* (July 3), became *Lady Macbeth of Mtensk* (page 14, G2, July 24).

● **22 January 2002**
Our efforts to spell *Lady Macbeth of Mtsensk* correctly continue. She appeared to come from Mtsenk on page 12, Saturday Review, January 19.

● **30 Jul 2001**
In a piece about the beer industry in Germany, page 24, Finance, July 25, Humorator became Humerator, Binding became Bundung, and Brau und Brunnen became Brau und Binnen.

● **1 Feb 2002**
In our report about the ICA, page 2, January 30, we referred to the famous knitter in *A Tale of Two Cities* as Madame Lafarge. She was Madame Defarge.

● **14 Jun 2002**
The acting chairman of the Press Complaints Commission is not George Pinker (Press glee over Blair's retreat, page 4, June 12). It is Professor Robert Pinker.

● **9 May 2003**
The chairman of the Press Complaints Commission is Sir Christopher Meyer and not Sir Peter Meyer (a column, page 5, G2, yesterday).

● **21 Aug 1998**
We spelt Morecambe, the town in Lancashire, wrong again on page 2, G2, yesterday. We often do.

Morec?mbe 10
H?ysham 12

● **17 Jul 2002**
In a column – My five tests for the euro, page 15, July 15 – the president of the European Central Bank, Wim Duisenberg, was inadvertently transposed into Dim Wuisenberg.

● **29 Jul 2002**
In a report Judges throw out Archer appeal, on page 2 of some editions, July 23, we had wrongly named,
one way or another, all three judges mentioned. Mr Justice Rose is Lord Justice Rose. Mr Justice Coleman is Mr Justice Colman. Mr Justice Burton is a judge who had nothing whatever to do with the case. Mr Justice Stanley Burnton, on the other hand, did. Apologies to everyone concerned.

OPEN DOOR
It's in its rightful place

Few things seem to provide readers of the Guardian with more amusement and irritation than the misplaced apostrophe – a word, the *Oxford English Dictionary* noted, purely as a matter of interest, that should really have three syllables rather than four. But let's not complicate matters.

It is difficult for those who (mistakenly) think they know all there is to be known about the apostrophe to avoid a tone of superiority. "Whatever the characteristics of *Howards End*, it does not have an apostrophe." That was a correction dictated by the Pooter in me. To tell you the truth I have no idea why Forster decided the apostrophe was not required.

These things are often a problem. We frequently misplace the apostrophe in The Queen's College, Oxford (we drop the definite article too, as a matter of Guardian style, even though it is part of the title and the college is listed alphabetically under T, at least in Oxford University's own roll of colleges). There is no guarantee that the apostrophe will appear in the right place in Queens' College, Cambridge. The apostrophe, it sometimes seems, is like an insect – an apostrofly – over the dining table, alighting where it will. If either name, Queen's or Queens', appears in the corrections column a dozen readers will accuse me of having an Oxbridge fixation.

The Queen's College, Oxford, explains on its own website (www.queens.ox.ac.uk) – no apostrophes there, you notice – that on its foundation in 1341 it was named in honour of Queen Philippa, a singular queen. Queens' College, Cambridge, well, where to start? The best thing to do is to turn to the page on the college's website entirely devoted to "The Apostrophe". Go to www.quns.cam.ac.uk and click on "Miscellaneous, historical and fun". It points out that although everyone is told that the name is spelt with the apostrophe after the s because the college was founded by two queens, Margaret of Anjou in 1448 and Elizabeth Woodville in 1465, it is not quite that simple. "The use of the apostrophe in English to indicate the possessive is of no great antiquity. The earliest examples of the name of the College spelt with an apostrophe always have the apostrophe before the s. The first example of the name of the College spelt with an apostrophe after the s was in 1823 ..." The spelling changed officially from Queen's to Queens' in 1831 – but not without continuing argument.

"The formal corporate title of the College is now: The Queen's College of St Margaret and St Bernard, commonly called Queens' College, in the University of Cambridge ... The name of the college when qualified by the patron saints is spelt in the singular; the short-form name is spelt in the plural." So that clears that up.

This is esoteric. The most common form of the affliction is when to say it's and its. The briefest advice is perhaps to be found in *The Macmillan Good English Handbook* compiled by Godfrey Howard. "Its is the possessive form ('a book has its title on the cover'); it's is the contracted form of 'it is' (it's a good title for a book')."

It is so humiliatingly simple that it perhaps explains why a colleague, standing in for me one day last week, put a correction in the following form: "To our shame, we allowed this sentence in a reader's letter to appear uncorrected ... 'No tyrannical regime likes it when it's own citizens expose it's flaws'." On the same page towards the end of last week we identified a letter-writer as a "spokesperson on womens' rights". What, a reader asked, are womens?

I cannot recommend too highly the essay on the apostrophe in the *New Fowler's Modern English Usage*, as revised by RW Burchfield (Oxford) – delight and instruction from beginning to end.

And so we come to Wordsworth's apostrophe, the subject of a correction – driven by calls from a dozen of you – that now needs qualifying. Here's the correction that appeared on September 5: "In a report of the commemoration of Wordsworth's poem on Westminster Bridge ... we insinuated a Guardian apostrophe so that the view from the bridge became, 'A sight so touching in it's majesty.'" In fact, the reporter, Angelique Chrisafis, had successfully preserved the apostrophe where it appeared in the collection of Wordsworth's poems of 1807, and where it appears in the celebratory booklet "Earth has not any thing to shew more fair", published jointly by Shakespeare's Globe and the Wordsworth Trust.

No manuscript of the sonnet has survived in Wordsworth's hand. Did he place the apostrophe there, or was it an error in copying for the printer, or was it a random mark left by the apostrofly?

30 Sep 2002

SPORT

● 25 Nov 1999

In our article about the jockey Pat Eddery, page 33, November 23, we said he had ridden four Derby winners which we listed as: Grundy (1975), El Gran Senor (1984), Law Society (1985) and Commander In Chief (1993). The first one, Grundy, is correct. All the others are wrong. Eddery did ride both El Gran Senor and Law Society in the Derby in the years mentioned, but he came second on each occasion, not first. Commander In Chief did win the Derby in 1993, but it was not ridden by Eddery. It was ridden by Mick Kinane. Eddery in fact has ridden three Derby winners, not four. They are Grundy (1975) Golden Fleece (1982) and Quest for Fame (1990).

● 14 Feb 2000

In The Editor, page 3, February 11, we referred to the Six nations rugby [union] tournament in which we said "Wales thrashed France" – a possibly partisan way of interpreting the actual result: Wales 3, France 36.

● 14 Feb 2001

In our account of the Game Spirit Chase at Newbury, page 10, Sport, February 12, all references to Foundry Lane should have been changed to Function Dream.

● 3 Mar 2001

In a panel listing events that have been, or could be, postponed because of foot and mouth disease restrictions, we included the following: "Britain's oldest horse race, the Derby, faces cancellation for only the second time in its 480-year history." The Derby is not Britain's oldest horse race. Britannica.com, pointing out that the modern age of racing began with the inauguration of the English classic races, lists them in the following order: the St Leger, 1776; the Oaks, 1779; the Derby, 1780 (all of them falling a long way short of 480 years of age).

26 Jul 2001

Homophone corner from page 30, Sport, yesterday: "Sir Alex Ferguson last night unveiled a third ... player to compliment Ruud van Nistelrooy and Juan Veron ..."

29 Oct 2001

In a continuation of Online's lead feature, page 3, October 25, we said: "Chelsea is toying with the idea of offering whole games live several hours after the final whistle."

12 Aug 2003

In our interview with Sir Jack Hayward, the chairman of Wolverhampton Wanderers, page 20, Sport, yesterday, we mistakenly attributed to him the following comment: "Our team was the worst in the First Division and I'm sure it'll be the worst in the Premier League." Sir Jack had just declined the offer of a hot drink. What he actually said was "Our tea was the worst in the First Division and I'm sure it'll be the worst in the Premier League." Profuse apologies.

4 Oct 2002

In our Ryder Cup report, page 3, Sport, September 30, we misquoted Paul McGinley, attributing to him the following comment: "Sam Torrance has been a fantastic captain. We have eventually got them [the Americans] crying and I always said that we would eventually get there." What McGinley actually said was: "Sam Torrance has been a fantastic captain. We have eventually got him [Sam Torrance] crying [with emotion at the win] and I always said that we would eventually get there."

18 Oct 2002

We concluded our story about the athlete Paula Radcliffe, Superwoman must spare herself, page 24, October 15, with the words, "Yet no one could forgive Radcliffe for thinking she is superwoman after the year she has just had". We meant to say, "no one could blame her".

19 May 2003

In a note about the Giro d'Italia, Sport in brief, page 33, May 15, we said the race leader won the fifth stage "by the thickness of his yellow vest". The yellow vest is worn on the Tour de France. In Italy it is a pink vest (the maglia rosa).

● **31 Jul 2003**

A report about the Millennium Dome on our front page, July 29 (The dome: new delay, new doubts), referred to it as a potential venue for Olympic events in 2010. The Olympics, wherever they are held, will be in 2012.

● **3 Jul 2004**

In a panel, History of an extended family (about Australia), page 7, yesterday, we said Australia beat England at cricket for the first time at the Oval in 1882. That was the first time Australia beat England in England. The first victory was in Australia, in Melbourne, in 1877. The Bodyline series was not in 1929. It was in 1932-33.

● **18 Aug 2004**

In a report from Athens, page 3, Sport, August 14, we referred to the swift suspension of Ivan Slavkov, "the Bulgarian IOC member alleged in a BBC Panorama programme to have been prepared to accept a bride to vote for London's 2012 [Olympic] bid". The allegation concerned a bribe, not a bride.

● **11 Dec 2003**

A blurb at the top of page 31 yesterday read: "After the World Cup – Paterson and Michalak back among ordinary morals."

● **27 Aug 2004**

An explanation of yngling (What is yngling?) posted on our website on August 19, refers to a planning dinghy. That is a planing dinghy. Planing is when the boat lifts over its bow wave thus enhancing its speed.

● **14 Sep 2004**

A report of the World Cup qualifying match between Switzerland and the Republic of Ireland (page 35 of some early editions, September 9), referred in the headline to the "Swiss cheese defence", conceding in the text that both defences had "more holes than a slab of Gouda cheese". Gouda does not have holes and is Dutch, not Swiss. It was changed to Emmenthal for later editions.

GEOGRAPHY

17 Dec 1997
On a map on page 13, December 12, the word Cornwall was written across Devon.

8 Jan 1998
On the Analysis page, page 13, yesterday, we referred to Germany's Italian frontier. It does not have one.

10 Apr 1998
In a sidebar on page 9, G2, April 8, we described a cave in Derbyshire "with fantastic stagalmites and stagaltites" and added, "yes, I know its [sic] stalagmites and stalagtites – but our guide got it wrong". So did we. Stalagmite (the one that projects upwards) and stalactite (the one that hangs) are the right spellings.

19 Oct 1998
In a review of the film *Hamam: The Turkish Bath* (page 9, October 16), we inadvertently suggested that Istanbul was the capital of Turkey. It's still Ankara.

3 Nov 1998
A map on page 12 yesterday, accompanying an article headed, Palestinians thirsting for justice on tap, showed Syria in the place of Jordan.

28 Nov 1998
In a graphic, page 11, Sport, November 21, the River Wye missed Hereford by quite a long way.

24 Nov 1999
Vastogirardi, the village with a dwindling population in southern Italy, page 21, November 20, would be conspicuous rather than "anonymous amid the Pennine mountains". The spinal mountains of Italy are the Apennines.

16 May 2000
We moved mountains, page 13, yesterday, in a report headed Putin redraws the map of Russia. We, rather than the Russian president, placed the Urals 900 miles west of Moscow. They are, of course, east of Moscow.

2 Aug 2000

The cover story in G2, July 31, recounted life as a car salesman in Stevens Creek, California, a location which appeared in the piece as Stephen's Creek and Steven's Creek, both of which are wrong. A third version appeared in the standfirst heading on page 2, also wrong: Jacob's Creek.

3 Oct 2000

The hurricane warning, page 15, yesterday, covered the Yucatan peninsula, not peninsular (a word very rarely needed but often used).

30 Jan 2001

In a report headed £4.5bn on offer to revive rail service, page 13, January 25, we said, "Tourists pouring off the Channel ferries or approaching London on Eurostar from Paris or Brussels have expressed their shock at seeing such a rundown station [Clapham Junction] at the southern gateway to the capital," None of these services goes to or through Clapham Junction.

19 Apr 2001

Geography department (1): In Weatherwatch, page 16, April 17, Ahmadabad was placed in northeast India. It is a city in Gujarat, which is in west-central India.

Geography department (2): Cape Verde Islands (Paint it black, G2, page 14, April 16) lie 200 miles west of Senegal, in the Atlantic. We said they were 200 miles to the east, which would place them inland, on the border between Mali and Mauritania.

Geography department (3): If Childe Harold had travelled downstream on the Rhine from Königswinter (He wrote the poem, you see the sights, Travel, page 2, April 14) he would have ended up in Rotterdam instead of Koblenz. He would also have noticed that the lake in Hamburg is called Alster and not Alstadt, that Drachenfels has just one l, that Siebengebirge (the seven hills) are not Sibengerberge, and that Hatto was archbishop of Mainz, not Meinz.

6 Oct 2001

The map accompanying our report of the Russian airliner disaster, on the front page yesterday, was wrong in a number of important points. It showed Novosibirsk, the capital of Siberia, as a resort on the Black Sea. It showed Israel extending over Jordan, and Jordan in place of Iraq.

● 14 Mar 2002

From Country Diary, page 20, G2, yesterday: "This was the .moon, on the first spring tide, to summon up the Severn Boar, the wave which charges inland ..." [Severn Bore]

● 25 Mar 2002

In a piece, Mothers' pride, page 8 (Women), G2, March 21, we referred to a group of women who met in a village on the "Oxford/ Hertfordshire borders". Those counties do not have a common border.

● 15 Aug 2002

The Moldau river in the caption to a picture of Prague on the front page, August 13, is one with the Vltava, its Czech name, correctly used throughout the accompanying report. Moldau is the river's German name.

● 26 Aug 2002

There were several errors in the map accompanying our report Rush to the bank holiday sun, page 8, August 23. Devon was written across Dorset, Cornwall extended across Devon, and Southend was placed in the close vicinity of Clacton. Buxton found itself in the Lake District rather than the Peak District.

● 30 Aug 2002

It is regretted that on a picture spread purporting to show "images of global pollution", page 12 and 13, G2, yesterday, the dominant photograph was of the Blue Lagoon, the geothermal spa in Iceland. Far from being an image of pollution, the Blue Lagoon is a rightly famous example of the proper use of natural resources. Apologies.

● 7 Oct 2002

In an article on pages 16 and 17, Travel, September 28, we repeatedly misspelled Machynlleth (Machnylleth), and also spelt wrongly Llanwddyn (Llanwyddyn) and Vyrnwy (Vrynwy).

● 10 Oct 2002

In Pass Notes about Quaoar, page 4, G2, yesterday, we illustrated its size by comparing it with the Earth, which, we said, was "8,000 miles around". In fact, that is the diameter of Earth. It is about 25,000 miles in circumference.

● 22 Jan 2003

Egypt was represented twice in our front-page map, yesterday, showing the deployment of forces in the crisis over Iraq. In its southern representation it was occupying the position of Sudan.

21 Nov 2000

In a report headed Stranger than fiction, pages 2 and 3, G2, November 16, about Florida and its way with elections, we said that Carol Roberts, a member of the Palm Beach electoral board, was forced to step down after being charged with ballot-tampering. In fact, she defended herself against the charges and was vindicated. The attempt to unseat her was therefore unsuccessful.

In the same piece we said "a man in south-central Florida was charged with shooting his dog because he suspected it of being gay". The reporter who covered the case says the dog, a neutered Yorkshire terrier-poodle cross, was not shot but struck on the head with a plastic piece of a vacuum cleaner, because the owner believed he was attempting an unnatural act with a Jack Russell terrier. The blow fractured the dog's skull and a local veterinary surgeon put the dog down. The dog's owner was sentenced to six months in prison, a term now nearing its end. Finally, Ocala is in north-central Florida, rather than south-central [Thanks to Rick Cundiff of the Ocala Star-Banner].

22 Jan 2003

In our map of the United States, page 64, Education, yesterday, the state of Maine was labelled New Brunswick. New Brunswick is not in the US. It is a province of Canada. In the same map we misspelled Wisconsin.

14 May 2004

Turkey was inadvertently placed in the Arab world in a caption, page 6, G2, yesterday.

8 Jul 2004

It is the river Esk at Whitby (Whitby marina plan sails into stormy waters, page 10, July 6), not the Eske. The Eske is in Ireland. The artist quoted in the report is John Freeman, not Freemen.

15 Jul 2004

We included Omaha among a list of states in a report about roads and forests in the US, page 12, yesterday. Omaha is not a state. We meant to say Montana.

● **31 Aug 2004**

A map accompanying a story about extreme weather conditions (The planet goes haywire, G2, August 27, page 11), placed Serbia in Russia. We meant to say Siberia.

● **28 Sep 2004**

In a report, page 12, Education, September 21, we said that a book aimed at raising Aids awareness among children in South Africa was to be translated into Corsa. That would be Xhosa.

● **30 Sep 2004**

In our G2 cover story yesterday we said the Orcadian farmer, George Drever, left Westray for "Orkney mainland (that is to say the island of Orkney ...)." There is no island of Orkney. Orkney refers to a group of more than 70 islands (17 of them inhabited), not one of which is called Orkney. The group may also be called the Orkney Islands, or (disliked by Orcadians) the Orkneys (*Collins*). The name of the largest island is Mainland. It is also referred to as "the" Mainland, or Orkney Mainland or Mainland Orkney. You can live in Orkney but not on Orkney. Mainland in the quoted passage above should have been capitalised.

● **2 Oct 2004**

Cagliari, the regional capital of Sardinia, became Calgary, in our report about fertility treatment, A matter of life and death, pages 8 and 9, G2, yesterday.

● **15 Oct 2004**

The answer given for the clue "River flowing through Heidelberg" in the Wordsquare on the Pyrgic Puzzles page in Weekend, October 9, was Elbe. That river rises in the Czech Republic and goes nowhere near Heidelberg. It is the Neckar that flows through Heidelberg.

● **16 Oct 2004**

As several readers have pointed out, the Pyrgic Puzzles clue "River flowing through Heidelberg" (Corrections, yesterday) was cryptic, not geographical. The correct answer was indeed Elbe (as in HeidELBErg).

● **15 Dec 2004**

The state capital of Alaska is Juneau and not, as was stated in a brief Reuters news item, Anchorage (Weather halts oil spill clean-up, page 14, December 13).

OPEN DOOR
Barrack room blaggards

The Readers' Editor on... **minding the gap between English and Australian**

Last week we carried a note in our daily corrections column that perhaps now needs a clarification, if not a total withdrawal. A couple of days earlier on the front page of the paper we had published a story recording Churchill's victory in the BBC's search for the greatest ever Briton.

In it we said that at one stage Isambard Kingdom Brunel was leading, after "some vigorous barracking" for him (*for* him, please note) by Jeremy Clarkson.

This brought the following email: "Barrack means 'shout or jeer at (performers at cricket, etc.)' ... it is a transitive verb, requiring an object: 'the crowd barracked the England team'. This is not what Jeremy Clarkson did to Brunel."

The correction read: "Jeremy Clarkson did not engage in 'vigorous barracking' for Brunel ... Barrack: to criticise loudly or shout against (*Collins*)." This prompted an email from another reader: "If to barrack is 'to criticise loudly or shout against', would not someone who barracks for (and I emphasise 'for') another be criticising that person's opposition? This would explain the Australian usage of the word, where enthusiastic supporters unequivocally 'barrack for' their sports teams, in the main by deriding players of the opposition."

Prepare to dive. The writer of the front page report is, it turns out, Australian. My glossary of Australian English (given to me, helpfully, some time ago by a graduate of Monash University) says – between barbie (barbecue) and beanie (woolly hat) – barrack (for) (v): support (sports etc).

Collins, in fact, was consulted too hastily in support of the correction. The entry in my edition, noting its use in Australia and New Zealand, says, as its second definition: intransitive verb, followed by "for", to shout support (for). It then suggests an origin in northern Irish in the 19th century: to boast.

The great *Oxford English Dictionary* caught up with the relevant definition in its supplement of 1933 when it noted its origin in this usage as Australian: "To shout jocular or sarcastic remarks or words of advice as partisans for or against a person, esp a person, or side collectively, engaged in a contest." It suggests a link with the Australian and New Zealand slang word borak, perhaps from Aboriginal Australian, meaning nonsense or humbug.

One example from the *OED* of barracking for, before we rise to the surface again. It comes from the Melbourne Punch of 1890, "To use a football phrase, they all to a man 'barrack' for the British Lion." The next question is: should we have ruled out the use of the word in our report on the grounds that it is an "Australianism"? The answer is, possibly – in the way that we might have replaced an intrusive Americanism. (This posing and answering of one's own questions particularly irritates one reader). I find it difficult to barrack either for or against it.

Was the use of "blaggard" in a letter to the editor last week a similar phenomenon, denoting a spelling that is legitimate in its context, this time Irish English, but for which no authority is to be found in the English dictionary? The letter writer was quoting his father: "Football is a gentleman's game played by blaggards, rugby is a blaggard's game played by gentlemen and Gaelic football is a blaggard's game played by blaggards."

The spelling reproduces the pronunciation of black guard or blackguard, and the latter is the way in which it should normally be spelt. Modern dictionaries define it as "scoundrel" or something similar. This is the first definition too of Eric Partridge in *A Dictionary of Slang and Unconventional English* (I have the third edition, 1949, in front of me). He continues: "At first this was a collective noun: in the 16th and 17th centuries, the scullions of a great house from the later 16th century, the Devil's body-guard in the 17th century, the camp-followers in the 18th century, a body of attendants of black dress, race or character, or the underworld, esp the shoe-blacking portion thereof." Partridge points for further discussion of "this interesting word" to the SOD (his abbreviation for the *Shorter Oxford Dictionary*) and the *OED* itself. Blaggard, so far as I can see, nowhere appears.

2 Dec 2002

PLACE

Place

20 Feb 1998
A Country Diary, page 16, February 17, was headed, Heald Green, Cheshire. Heald Green is in Stockport, Greater Manchester. The error was caused by nostalgia.

25 Aug 2000
A comment piece yesterday, page 23, had Winston Churchill reflecting on his time as a "profoundly unsuccessful schoolboy at Marlborough". He went to Harrow.

11 Oct 2000
The Glasgow thoroughfare referred to in a leader, page 21, yesterday, is Sauchiehall, not Sauciehall.

23 Mar 2001
The world's first McDonald's hotel is not at Rümland in Switzerland (page 14, March 16), or Ramlüng (pages 6, G2, March 19), but Rümlang.

25 Apr 2002
In the picture on page 7, yesterday, Picasso was shown on the beach at Juan-les-Pins, not St Juan Les Pin.

11 Jul 2002
The Pitt Rivers museum was placed in Cambridge instead of Oxford due to an editing error in an article about the shrunken heads and other body parts residing in British museums, Bones of contention, page 15, July 9.

29 Jul 2002
Queen's College, Cambridge, in the report about Ofcom, page 19, July 23, should be Queens' College, Cambridge – not to be confused with the Queen's College, Oxford.

14 Aug 2002
In the obituary of American neo-Nazi William Pierce (page 20, July 25) we said that the former Ku Klux Klan leader, David Duke, was from Tennessee. He is from Louisiana.

● **10 Feb 2003**

In our obituary of the film distributor Kenneth Rive, page 22, February 3, we inserted the incorrect intelligence that he was born in Germany. In fact, he was born in Canonbury in north London.

● **18 Feb 2003**

In our report of the Crystal Palace-Leeds United match, page 2, Sport, yesterday, we suggested that Hayden Mullins was Australian. He is not. He was born in Reading.

● **1 Aug 2003**

The capital of Ghana (Accra) may be called the Ghanaian capital, but not the Ghanese capital (We're dying here ... etc) page 10, July 30).

● **25 Sep 2003**

Sigmund Freud lived at Maresfield Gardens in north London, not Masefield Road as stated on page 29, Saturday review, September 20, Sigmund's London.

● **18 Oct 2003**

Yesterday's leader, page 17, erred in saying trains no longer stop at Carnforth station, site of the classic film, *Brief Encounter*. They do.

● **19 Oct 1999**

The building illustrating Simon Hoggart's Diary, page 12, Saturday Review, October 16, was not Cheltenham Town Hall, as the caption suggested it might be. It was Boots the Chemist.

● **09 Aug 2004**

The place shown in a photograph on page 14 of a supplement, Greece revisited, published with the Guardian, August 6, is not in fact in Greece. It is the Anassa resort and spa in Cyprus.

● **13 Nov 2004**

There may be a gap between Mayfair and Middlesbrough, but not between "Mayfair and Middlesborough", page 4, G2 in China, November 8.

● **05 Jan 2005**

In a report about a portrait of Charlotte Brontë, page 13, January 1, we misspelled throughout the piece and in a caption the name of the village of Haworth (not Howarth), where the family lived.

MATHS

Maths

16 Sep 1998

In an article in Guardian Weekend, headed The god of fast things, Page 41, September 12, we suggested that at the speed of light you could make 11,160 return journeys from Victoria to Brighton in 60 minutes. In fact, you would only need about six seconds.

29 Sep 1999

A reference to the "122 mile journey" of the Mars Climate Orbiter, from Earth to Mars, page 8, September 24, should have read 122 million miles.

25 Oct 1999

In a report, Potato seeks recipe for kitchen cred, page 4, October 21, we said: "The microwave may be helping to stave off competition by cutting baking times for potatoes by up to a 10th ..." That should have been to a 10th, or to put it another way, we could have said the microwave cuts baking times by up to 90%.

20 Mar 2000

In a piece, Shark suits give swimmers speed, page 8, March 17, we said it was claimed that swimmers using the suits – which mimic the qualities of a shark's skin – had "increased their overall times by 3%". Their speed was increased, and their overall times reduced.

27 Nov 2000

In our report, Reckless bush clearance may cost Australia the earth, page 21, November 24, we referred to a couple who acquired 790 hectares of land and said this was equivalent to 320 acres. We should have said they had acquired 320 hectares which was equivalent to 790 acres.

2 Apr 2001

In a report about the "euthanasia drug", pentobarbitone sodium, page 4, March 30, we made several references to 100 millimetre bottles. We meant to refer to millilitres.

15 Aug 2001

The Caribbean island of Nelson, Exiled to paradise, Saturday Review, page 3, August 11, was described as "a square mile in circumference". The area of the island may be one square mile but its circumference has to be a linear measure, which would be just over 3.5 miles.

9 May 2002

In a piece, Next challenge in space: hitching a ride on a sunbeam, page 20, May 6, we said: "Under the pressure of the sun's rays, the spacecraft would begin accelerating at only millimetres per second, every second. But in just a day, an acceleration of 1mm per second would build up to 100 metres per second." We should have said "... an acceleration of 1mm per second per second would build up to a velocity of 100 metres per second".

21 May 2004

In a report from Cannes, Kiss and make up, page 11, G2, May 19, we referred to Truffaut's film *Fahrenheit 561*. It was actually *Fahrenheit 451*.

31 May 2002

Mythematics corner: The Elsewhere column startled its readers, page 22, yesterday, by stating there are 56 quarters to one hundredweight. There are four quarters to a hundredweight (but there are 56 pounds in half a hundredweight).

2 Oct 2002

In a panel headed, The numbers game, reporting conflicting estimates of the size of the anti-war march in London, we said the organisers claimed at least 400,000, a figure calculated by multiplying the time it took the march to pass through Whitehall, 4hrs 40mins, by 1,000, the estimated number of marchers passing a given point per minute. Using those figures, the total would come to 280,000: 4hrs 40mins = 280 minutes x 1,000 = 280,000 (a point about our figures, not the size of the march).

20 Nov 2002

An article, Now for the good news, page 6, Education, yesterday, began: "Back in the days when money was money and you got a full 244 pennies to the pound ..." In fact, there were 240 pennies to the pound.

22 Nov 2002

In our report, Support for royals plunges to record low, page 1, November 20, we said, "Labour voters are equally split, with 36% opposed and 36% against." We meant they were split equally at 36% for and 36% against.

4 Dec 2003

Haweswater, in the Lake District, holds rather more than the 84,630 litres we gave it in a report, Request to drain water from Lakes, page 12, yesterday. That figure is its capacity in billions of litres.

9 Dec 2003

An editing error giving miles instead of metres (for the abbreviation m) made nonsense of a report headed Europe and US clash on satellite system (page 4, early editions, page 11, later editions, yesterday). It caused us to say that Europe's planned navigation system to rival the US one would be accurate to within 4 miles.

12 Dec 2003

A sevenfold increase in the number of women dying of liver disease (A whole lotta bottle, G2, page 8, yesterday) was translated into a 700% increase in a picture caption. A sevenfold increase is 600%.

28 Jan 2004

A headline reading: 43% of jurors fail to grasp details, page 13, yesterday, misconstrued the text. That said that 43% of jurors claimed they understood everything that was happening.

26 Mar 2004

In a report, Wind farms planned for oil rig, page 16, Business, March 24, we said the generator required would weigh as much as a jumbo jet: 1,300 tonnes. According to Boeing, the maximum take-off weight for a 747 is around 400 tonnes. An unladen 747 weighs approximately 150 tonnes. It can carry its own weight in fuel and another 100 tonnes or so of cargo.

24 Jun 2004

We exaggerated the beer consumption of a tenanted pub in a panel, Landlords' laments, page 24, yesterday. We meant to say 210 barrels (a year), not 210,000.

26 Jul 2004

A report of the return of the Globe players to Hampton Court Palace with a production of *Measure for Measure* claimed it was first performed there 500 years ago. This fact was repeated in the headline. The story explained that the performance took place before the new King James at Christmas and New Year 1603-04, which is 400 years ago (After 500 years, Globe's players return to perform at the palace, page 3, July 19).

● 7 Aug 2004

The graph accompanying our report on the increase in personal debt contained misleading figures on its vertical axis. Each figure had an extra zero, eg 80,000 was expressed as 80,0000 (£1,000,000,000,000: Household debt breaks the one trillion barrier, page 3, July 30).

● 2 Nov 2004

Mythematics: a panel about Florida on page 1 yesterday put President Bush's majority there in the 2000 election at "537 – 0.00009% of voters". This would mean that there were 600 million voters in Florida. As one reader pointed out: "That's quite a lot for a state with a population of only 17 million." The figure actually represented 0.009% of those who voted.

● 2 Nov 2004

An erroneous conversion was inserted into a report about Blenheim Palace on page 7 yesterday when it was described as a "5,000-hectare (2,000-acre) estate". The figure in brackets should have been 12,500 acres.

OPEN DOOR
A headline too far

The Readers' Editor on... **phrases that never fail to annoy**

Fowler, in his *Modern English Usage* (revised by RW Burchfield), third edition, 1998, is at his sniffiest on the subject. "A regrettable tendency has emerged in recent years, especially in non-standard English in Britain and abroad, to construe the verb with of." He is talking about the verb to bore, defined in James Murray's *Oxford English Dictionary*, as "to weary by tedious conversation or simply by the failure to be interesting".

Fowler says: "The normal constructions are with with or with by." He, or rather his successor Mr Burchfield, gives a number of examples of the [mis]use of the verb with "of". Remarkably, none are taken from the 200 or so occurrences in the Guardian over the past few years.

"I'm so bored of him. He's lost his virility" (C Phipps, 1989) is one of Burchfield's examples. He also quotes Iona Opie, 1993, presumably from her *The People in the Playground*: "[Children] use the preposition 'of' in an unorthodox way: 'I'm bored of this,' they say (taking the construction from 'tired of')."

I hope I am not boring you with this. Several of you always write when "bored of" occurs in the text of a story. Last week rather more than several of you wrote. "I noticed an article was topped by the headline 'Bored of fashion'. There seems to be an increased use of the word 'of' to follow bored ... but this is the first time I have seen it used in a headline ... To me it always sounds wrong. Is it one of those things that used to be wrong but is now becoming acceptable because more and more people do it?"

No, it is not acceptable (yet). The following appeared in the Corrections and Clarifications column: "The headline 'Bored of fashion', supported by a couple of similar references in the text, caused an understandable gnashing of teeth. The style guide says: bored with, by, not bored of. The confusion perhaps comes from the legitimate 'tired of'."

It was not, in fact, the first time the construction had appeared in a headline. Here is a note from the corrections column just a year earlier: "Language department: a headline 'Adam Cooper left the Royal Ballet because he was bored of dancing the classics'. The construction 'bored of' is banned by our style guide which, quite rightly, prefers bored with or by. (He was tired of dancing the classics and bored by doing so.)"

It is not just us or you. Quite a recent book, *Mind the Gaffe: The Penguin Guide to Common Errors in English* by RL Trask (Penguin 2001) says: "Bored

– The established expression is bored with, not bored of, which should be avoided in careful writing."

These are little things made bigger when they creep into headlines. Even so they rank very low on the scale of journalistic sins. Much more annoying for many of you are headlines based on cliché quotes: A man for all seasons; Not waving but drowning; A (something) too far; Things fall apart. (I am pretty sure I have used them all in a tight corner.)

In this category, one thing guaranteed to upset some of you is the [mis]use of the phrase from the Gospel According to Saint Mark (King James Version): "10:13 And they brought young children to him, that he should touch them: and his disciples rebuked those that brought them. 10:14 But when Jesus saw it, he was much displeased, and said unto them, Suffer the little children to come unto me, and forbid them not: for of such is the kingdom of God." A modern English version puts the relevant part like this: "Let the little children come to me and do not try to stop them."

A cliché is a cliché and perhaps it is one of its characteristics that it is detached from its original meaning. In *Collins*, the Guardian's preferred dictionary, to be consulted in the absence of any note in the style guide, as in this case, it is the fifth definition. Suffer: (archaic), to permit someone to do something, "suffer the little children to come unto me".

The following headline, which appeared this week, "Suffer the little children – Sats revolt looms", prompted this slightly weary protest from a reader: "Could someone please (please) tell Guardian writers to avoid the vulgar misuse of Mark 10:14 ... Can this injunction not be put on some message board or something – for all to see."

There are two principal objections to it: one, that it is a disrespectful mucking about with a resonant phrase from the King James Version, and two, that it simply appears much too often. Fairly recently we have had, "Suffer little children – Leahy tells how Tesco got to be open all hours" and "Suffer little children" on a report about rising costs of daycare for working parents. Sometimes the ironic intent is more apparent than others. The long-suffering reader would be happier if we abandoned it.

17 May 2003

ANIMALS

16 Mar 1998

On page 6, March 12, in a report headed, Search for "ferret bounty" victims leaves Shetland islanders baffled, we described ferrets as rodents. They are not. They are *mustelidae* (order *carnivora*).

14 Sep 2004

We spoiled the punchline in the joke used to trail the C4 programme, *Funny Already: The History of Jewish Comedy* (page 63, the Guide, September 11). We told it like this: "What's the difference between a rottweiler and a Jewish mother? A Jewish mother will eventually let go ..." The punchline, as many readers pointed out, should read: "A rottweiler will eventually let go."

16 Jun 1998

The ethnic Albanians fleeing Kosovo shown in a photograph (page 20, June 13) were riding mules, not donkeys, as the caption wrongly stated.

7 Mar 2000

One of the pictures illustrating our piece about the gorillas of the Uganda/Congo border area, pages 6 and 7, Travel, March 4, purported to show Dian Fossey with two gorillas. In fact it showed Birute Galdikas with orang-utans in Borneo (as one reader observed, wrong person, wrong animal, wrong continent). The picture belonged to a set wrongly identified and filed in 1998.

4 Nov 2000

The chimpanzees on the front of Science, November 2, were orang-utans.

15 Nov 2001

The cat identified as an Abyssinian, page 47, Weekend, was, in fact, a chocolate tabby-point Siamese. Siamese have blue eyes, Abyssinians do not.

6 Dec 2001

The skink is not a rodent, it is a reptile (One family and other animals, page 1, early editions, December 4).

30 Jan 2003

It is not the gall bladder that provides buoyancy in fishes but the swim bladder, and it is this that is absent in sharks (Learning: Shark attack, page 72, Education, January 28).

20 Feb 2003

The turtle shown in a picture to illustrate a report, Turtle hurtles towards extinction, and captioned "The body of a leatherback sea turtle washed up in Costa Rica ...", page 11, yesterday, was farther from extinction than we indicated. It was, in fact, alive, as the trail in the sand left by it as it returned to the sea clearly showed.

25 Feb 2003

The blurb of page 1 of The Editor, February 22, for its report on the proliferation of the Kamchatka crab, said: Eight legs bad, Stalin's hordes are invading Europe. In fact, crabs have 10 legs, the two front ones modified as pincers.

3 Apr 2003

The Stellar sea lions of Alaska mentioned in Pick of the day, page 24, G2, April 1, are in fact Steller's sea lions – named after the 18th-century German naturalist George Steller.

18 Apr 2003

The "equine statue of Saddam" in Tikrit's main square should have been described as an equestrian one, unless withering insult was intended. Equine: resembling a horse – *Collins* (A moment of pure Hollywood in the town of a thousand Saddams, page 3, April 15).

5 Oct 2004

An observation of "cows calving and ... mares fowling", page 13, October 2, was only half right. The mares were foaling.

24 Nov 2004

The photograph of a fish firing a waterjet from its mouth to bring down an insect from a leaf was an archerfish and not, as we said, an anglerfish (Natural defences, Life, page 6, November 18).

HEALTH

● **18 Nov 1997**

An item in News in Brief, Page 6, November 13, made an incorrect reference to "seasonal adjustment disorder". It should have said, "seasonal affective disorder", often referred to by the acronym SAD.

● **23 Nov 1997**

In the Analysis page about multiple births (Page 17, November 21), in a reference to the Dionne quintuplets, we said: "It was a miracle that they had survived ... since they each weighed less than 14 pounds when they were born ..." It should have said "since together they weighed less than 14 pounds".

● **23 Sep 1998**

In a review of *The Anatomist* by Federico Andahazi, page 10, Saturday Review, September 19, we said the book was "factually based" on the life of Mateo Renaldo Colombo, "the anatomist who discovered and named ... the clitoris". This is not correct. The clitoris and its function were well known to the Romans and referred to in both their popular and medical literature.

● **20 Oct 1998**

The disease of the liver referred to in the article, May we have the pleasure? (page 1, Saturday section, October 17), should have been cirrhosis not sclerosis.

● **30 Mar 1999**

The dancer described near the beginning of the article, The politics of dancing, page 30, Guardian Weekend, March 27, did not have exfoliated genitalia, but depilated genitalia (having lost her hair rather than layers of skin).

● **14 Sep 1999**

Our graphic anatomy lesson, Abdominal pregnancy, page 4, September 11, was misleading in a number of points. Eggs are fertilised in the fallopian tube, not the womb. The stomach cavity should, strictly, have been called the abdominal cavity. The piece itself should have spoken of the inability to remove the placenta from the abdomen, not the stomach.

18 Apr 2000

In Parents, page 11, G2, April 12, a book on eating disorders by Joan Purgold was listed as *The Lingering Melody*. The correct title is *The Lingering Malady*.

26 Aug 2000

A Health article, G2, page 10, August 23, said swimming helped reduce "high blood pressure and hypertension". They mean the same thing.

3 Nov 2000

Not a homophone, from page 31, November 1, Market forces, "In Glaxo's case it was further problems with its controversial treatment for irritable bowl syndrome ..."

2 Mar 2001

In an article about gap years, Education, pages 12 and 13, February 27, we included in a survival guide for students working abroad the advice to "get vaccinated against illnesses like TB and malaria". There is no vaccination against malaria.

9 Feb 2002

The surgical removal of the clitoris is a clitoridectomy, not a clitorectomy (page 4, G2, yesterday).

2 May 2003

Our sketch, page 2, April 30, referred to "doctors who have been struck off by the BMA". The BMA is a professional association. It cannot strike off anyone. That is a responsibility of the General Medical Council, the statutory regulatory body.

14 Jan 2004

We captioned a photograph with our radio notes, page 20, G2, yesterday, "The syphilis virus". Syphilis is caused by a bacterium, not a virus.

5 Aug 2004

In a column headed Save us from the armchair generals, page 5, G2, the writer, having referred to the matter of gay people in the armed forces, noted that "former admiral of the fleet Peter Hill-Norton, has gone a little quiet on the subject ..." That is because he died in May this year.

19 Jun 2004

In a short piece considering why an Indian holy man who rolls rather than walks never appears to get dizzy, page 2, Life, June 10, we explained, "Just as some people who have become proficient in mediation can actually slow down their heart rate, perhaps he [avoids dizziness] by simply shutting down his response mechanism." Mediators will find that meditation helps too.

30 June 2004

A column of facts about Iraq on the front page of some editions yesterday referred to the availability of "portable water". Potable, that should have been (drinkable).

20 Oct 2004

In Leaked report damns passive smoking, page 7, yesterday, we quoted the general secretary of the TUC saying: "Half-measures will not save the 700 employers who die every year due to passive smoking at work." What she actually said was "700 employees".

13 Nov 2004

We said in an article, West Midlands aims to buff up its image, page 9, October 27, that a regional triumph was "the discovery of Gamgee tissue (now known as cotton wool)". Gamgee tissue, which was invented rather than discovered, is a wound dressing made up of a thick layer of cotton wool with a cover of woven gauze on either side. Dr Sampson Gamgee, a consulting surgeon at Queens Hospital in Birmingham, was granted a patent in 1883.

24 Jan 2005

The man extolling the virtues of breast milk, mentioned in When is breast best?, page 9, G2, January 18, believed that it had given him remission from prostate cancer rather than prostrate cancer.

27 Jan 2005

In a brief item, BBC wrong to show clip, page 5, yesterday, we reported a decision by the BBC governors that it had been "inappropriate" to show a clip from a documentary on "sleeping sickness" in a Greatest TV Moments show. The documentary did not deal with sleeping sickness and the governors' ruling did not say that it had. It was about narcolepsy. They are not the same thing.

COUNTRYSIDE

16 Dec 1997

On the Analysis page (page 15, December 9), we referred to "a further 1.5 billion (cattle) slaughtered as a precaution" in the BSE crisis. It should have read, 1.5 million.

23 Dec 1997

A panel, Beef facts, which accompanied a report on page 8 yesterday, was sexually confused. It referred to beef cows, instead of beef cattle. It described heifers as male calves, instead of female cattle which have not calved. It described steers as female calves, instead of castrated males, or bullocks.

26 Jan 1998

There were two errors in Country Diary, page 18, January 22. We referred to the "globally important flower country" when we should have said flow country. We said sand martins still occasionally nest in Smoo Cave. The writer meant to say house martins.

6 Nov 2000

Our reference to the national "herd" of sheep, a leader, page 23, November 2, should have been to the national flock.

6 Oct 2001

An article, Fowl play, on page 7, G2, yesterday, about pheasants was illustrated by a man banging away on a grouse moor.

21 Jan 2002

An article headed Marie Skinner had a farm, page 8, Women, January 17, produced a crop of errors. It referred to bone drafts and skin drafts, instead of grafts; it had escaliered trees instead of espaliered; someone was bailing rather than baling hay; it spoke of tennant farmers not tenant ...

20 Mar 2002

In a Country Diary, Branching out, page 16, G2, March 18, we gave the impression that the blackthorn tree produces damsons. Bitter experience confirms that it produces the sloe.

8 Jun 2000

Our blurb for the Channel 5 programme *Naked Jungle*, page 24, G2, June 6, suggested, "Keith Chegwin hosts the naked gameshow for naturalists." Naturists, in fact, whatever their interests.

22 Apr 2002

In a report, Cows forced to fly after hoofing it to island, page 10, April 19, we said "The Charolais, a breed [of cattle] that dates back to jurassic times ..." That would suggest that cattle were domesticated millions of years before the more likely date of 7,000 to 8,000 years ago. The Charolais breed dates from the 18th century.

27 Jul 2002

English Nature have asked us to point out that the mole cricket shown being eaten by a visitor to Liverpool museum in a picture on page 6, July 23, was not the English native species which is very rare and legally protected.

12 Jan 2004

The photograph on page 11, January 9, did not show almond blossom, as the caption suggested. It was cherry blossom, *Prunus subhirtella autumnalis*.

14 May 2004

The wheat, illustrated on page 2, Life, yesterday, is in fact barley.

30 June 2004

In an article about the early spider orchid, page 18, June 23, we mistakenly described the later spider orchid. The early variety has a brown flower with green wings. The late one has purple wings.

4 Sep 2004

The flower in the photograph of the San Salvador Monument to Memory and Truth was a hibiscus and not, as stated, a carnation (Gone but not forgotten, page 22, September 1).

CLASSICS

28 Jul 1998

We mixed up Aristarchus and Eratosthenes in a feature about the archaeology of Alexandria (Guardian Higher Education, page iv, July 14). It was Aristarchus of Samos who proposed that the Earth went round the Sun, and Eratosthenes who calculated the roundness of the Earth.

10 Dec 1998

The author of *School Britannia*, page 4, G2, yesterday, was wrong to call himself (and so were we to let him), "an old alumni of a public school". He is a singular alumnus.

3 Feb 1999

In our leader, Latin judgments, page 17, February 1, calling for a simplification of the language used in court, we tripped slightly in our own use of Latin. *Pendent lite* should have been *pendente lite*, and we should have referred to loquitur, not loquitors.

30 Mar 1999

Fiat volunta stua, in the Face to Faith column, page 23, March 27, should have been *Fiat voluntas tua*: "Thy will be done."

30 Aug 1999

It is intercrural copulation rather than intercural copulation in which men are depicted on Greek vases, bringing themselves to orgasm with the aid of a youth's clenched thighs, page 23, August 26, an article headed Deviance, if you like.

30 Nov 1999

In our review of the Channel 4 programme, *The Kid in the Corner*, page 22, G2, November 25, we said, "[his] mother ... confided to her shrink that he 'kicked and kicked and kicked' right through pregnancy, so she knew what kind of succubus to expect." She would, in that case, have been surprised to give birth to a boy. Succubus: a female demon fabled to have sexual intercourse with sleeping men. Incubus: a demon believed in folklore to lie upon sleeping persons, esp to have sexual intercourse with sleeping women (both definitions, *Collins Millennium*).

● **20 Jan 2000**

Apologies to readers of early editions, January 17, whose attention was drawn, page 10, to the "huge Ironic columns" of Manchester City Art Gallery. The Ionic columns were back in place for later editions.

● **23 Aug 2000**

The Roman emperor Claudius could not have patronised the Colosseum (Passnotes yesterday, G2, page 3), as he died in 54AD, roughly two decades before it was built under the emperor Titus Flavius Vespasianus, rendered Vespasian in English. The Byron quotation given ("When falls the Coliseum, Rome shall fall / And when Rome falls – the world") should have been assigned to *Childe Harold's Pilgrimage*.

● **5 Apr 2001**

In an article, Our survey said ..., pages 8 and 9, G2, April 2, we suggested that the lighthouse at "Athens harbour" was one of the wonders of the world. It was not, but the lighthouse at Alexandria was. Here is the list: The great pyramid of Giza, the hanging gardens of Babylon, the statue of Zeus at Olympia, the temple of Artemis at Ephesus, the mausoleum at Halicarnassus, the Colossus of Rhodes, and the lighthouse of Alexandria.

● **13 Jul 2001**

In a report, Library is a closed book for schools, page 5, yesterday, we referred to "the Roman historian Herodotus". Herodotus was a Greek historian.

● **8 Aug 2001**

It is not correct to describe the Minotaur as "one of Europa's grandchildren", page 14, G2 Arts, July 25. The Minotaur was the offspring of Pasiphae, the wife of Europa's son, Minos, and a bull which Minos should have sacrificed to Poseidon. Minos, in any biological sense, had nothing to do with it.

● **19 Oct 2002**

The "incomprehensible form of Latin" to which we referred in a report headed Booker is "won" a week early, page 11, October 17, was, in fact, simply a version of *Lorem ipsem*, dummy copy used by designers and typesetters to stand until the real text is available. Its garbled form derives from Cicero's *de Finibus Bonorum et Malorum*.

28 Nov 2002

Neptune raised a trident rather than a triton (Glittering reunion: Duke's silver service on show, page 11, yesterday).

14 Jul 2003

In a note on Sounion beach, Attica, page 14, Travel, July 5, we said, "What makes this ... beach ... special is the Temple of Apollo ..." It is the Temple of Poseidon, not Apollo.

7 Aug 2004

Dr Armand D'Angour, the author of the Pindaric ode quoted in English translation on page 10 yesterday (Oxford pays its debt to ancients in Pindaric song), has asked us to make it clear that he composed it in ancient Greek. More precisely it was composed in the Doric dialect used by Pindar, and in the complex dactylo-epitrite metre he favoured.

17 Aug 2004

The location of the observation by Eratosthenes that he cast no shadow at noon on the summer solstice was Syene (now Aswan in Egypt) and not Cyrene (now Shahhat in Libya). He was, however, born in Cyrene in 276BC (A point of inspiration, page 23, August 5).

1 Sep 2004

Calypso was the sea nymph who fell in love with Odysseus and kept him for seven years, promising him immortality and eternal youth if he would stay with her. In yesterday's radio review we mistakenly said it was Cyclops, the one-eyed giant (An epic undertaking, G2, page 20).

20 Jan 2005

The name of the city of Naples is derived from the Greek Neapolis (new town) not, as we said in a leader, from Neopolis (Herculaneum: Buried masterpieces, page 21, January 18).

OPEN DOOR
A penguin in Weimar

The Readers' Editor on... amiable encounters of the insignificant kind

A reader writes: "I am very disappointed and angry with you for refusing to publish my correction to a point made by Smallweed on the first Saturday of November. He said, inter alia, that Monmouthshire had always been part of England, a mistake also made in the *Statesman's Year Book*.

"In 1536, the English parliament passed an act attaching Monmouthshire to Oxford ..." And so on, not omitting references to Henry IV, Owain Glyndwr and Henry VIII. The point is conceded and would have been even without the distress registered in the reader's final sentence: "I buy my copy and I sent you two letters on this subject."

This was just one of the many corrections we failed to make during the year, omissions for which, in the spirit of the season, we ask forgiveness.

Here are some more: "The caption under the picture of Robert Macfarlane says he is 'in the quadrangle of Emmanuel College, Cambridge'. Cambridge colleges have courts, not quadrangles, and Emmanuel has several courts, not just one."

A reader, writing at the beginning of the year to instruct me on the difference between envy and jealousy ("What I find fascinating is that while envy is one of the seven deadly sins, jealousy is not"), began his letter: "I realise of course that this is being unbelievably pedantic ..."

Believe me, there is nothing unbelievable about it.

Railways quickly uncover the pedant in us: "Trains don't have undercarriages – aircraft do. There is a word for what trains run on, but I'm not going to tell you what it is, as you'd then promptly use it for aircraft or bicycles or something."

Among the many emails pointing out that we had said Weiner for Weimar was this one: "In an article on Robert Mugabe you referred to the Weiner Republic. Stood out like a sore thumb. Kind regards, Danny Weiner."

A reader wrote from Totnes, enclosing a cutting: "This is my (perhaps the) first-ever sighting of a greengrocer's apostrophe in the Guardian." (Can he have been paying attention?) The passage read: "Americans are suckers for pageantry and the media was happy to show shots of [President George Bush] surveying a row of busby's or chatting with the Queen."

Pedantry is yet to tighten its grip on this reader. Busby's should be busbies, or rather bearskins, and media (the word) is plural, so the media were happy, not was happy. You see how infectious a disease it is.

Readers do not confine their scrutiny to the editorial parts of the Guardian. Here is the reply to a reader from the department that deals with Guardian offers: "Thank you for your email regarding the photograph of penguins in the Norwegian Coastal Voyage insert which ran on Saturday. You are quite right in pointing out that penguins do not live in the regions featured in the insert and I apologise if this photograph misled you in any way. We ran a similar insert last year which featured a cruise to the Chilean fjords and Antarctica, where penguins can be found, and the picture was left in by mistake."

A reader of Guardian Unlimited, the online Guardian, wrote to object to the phrase "shaven-headed oafs" who had, in the words of the report, spat abuse at anti-racism protesters. "Now this may seem a trivial point but what has the haircut of anyone got to do with [it]? If these 'oafs' had all had long hair or curly perms would your reporter have commented on their hair then? Is this hairist?" (No mention of the injunction, one that I am often tempted to utter, "Keep your hair on".)

Other newspapers are occasionally quoted at us in frustration: "Regarding Gozo, I wrote on November 23 to point out that 'driving is on the right' is wrong. No reaction, I think. Tuesday December 9's Financial Times in its Malta supplement says, 'As in the UK, cars drive on the left'. Nuff said?" A point in passing: other newspapers make mistakes, too.

Correspondence of the kind quoted runs like a cool (fairly cool) stream through the rugged territory of corrections. Most of our arguments are amiable. To quote from the Everyman edition of *The Complete Works of Montaigne*: "When someone opposes me, he arouses my attention, not my anger. I go to meet a man who contradicts me, who instructs me. The cause of truth should be the common cause for both."

Or, on the same note, this exchange between Corporal Trim and his master, Uncle Toby, from Sterne's *Tristram Shandy*: "Now if I might presume, said the corporal, to differ from your honour – Why else do I talk to thee, Trim, said my Uncle Toby, mildly."

20 Dec 2003

BIRDS

Birds

15 Jan 1998

One of our leading articles (page 14, January 12), began, "As blue tits dive into the hedge to build their nests ..." Blue tits do not build nests in hedges. They prefer holes in tree trunks, amongst other locations.

26 Jan 1998

Pass Notes (page 3, G2, January 21), suggested that the Great Bustard that is preserved in a glass case in Trowbridge Museum, Wiltshire, was the only such specimen in the United Kingdom. There are four mounted Great Bustards in Ipswich Museum, two of which are believed to have been native Suffolk birds.

29 Jan 1998

The Great Bustard, Pass Notes, G2, January 21, a further correction (see Corrections, January 26). There is no Great Bustard in Trowbridge Museum but there are four specimens in Salisbury Museum.

2 Feb 1998

An article headed, Birds on a wire, G2 page 19, January 29, contained the following:
" ... birds left in the nets for long fade fast in climactic extremes". It should have said climatic. In the same piece the icterine warbler was misspelt.

11 Dec 1998

The ducks illustrating Notes & Queries, page 17, G2, December 9, were geese.

20 Jan 1999

Bird-watching: The bird which appeared in the Guardian on January 15 as a garden warbler (with an article about Messiaen's interest in birdsong), then in the Corrections column on January 16 as a song thrush, has now been conclusively identified as a brown thrasher.

3 Feb 1999

The "finely observed" peacocks we used as an example of the work of Sheila Hawkins to illustrate her obituary, page 19, January 30, were not peacocks but lyrebirds (*Menura novaehollandiae*).

● 2 Apr 1999

The birds' eggs seized by police (News in brief, page 9, March 31) were recovered from houses in Brixham, in Devon, not Brixton.

● 12 Feb 2000

We were mistaken to refer to the "hummingbird-infested tropical shrubs of Sydney" in a diary, page 12, Saturday Review, February 5. According to *Britannica* there are about 320 species of small birds that qualify for the name, but all in the New World (mostly South America), and none in Australia.

● 24 Oct 2000

The bird captioned "Nightingale: invisible", page 7, G2, yesterday, is visibly a skylark, as the caption supplied to us clearly said.

● 12 Mar 2003

An Indian bird pictured in The Editor (page 22, March 23) was controversially described by the agency that provided it as a blue hummingbird seen in a New Delhi park. The hummingbird (*Trochilidae*) is a native of the American continent and the blue throated hummingbird

(*Lampornis clemenciae*) is restricted to south-eastern Arizona, southwestern New Mexico and west Texas. The bird in the picture was a male purple sunbird (*Nectarinia asiatica*), a widespread resident in India.

● 14 Jul 2003

The mythical creature with an eagle's head and wings and a lion's body is a griffin or gryphon, but the bird of prey species, *Gyps fulvus*, is the griffon vulture, and not the griffin vulture as we had it all through an article, Return of the vulture, page 8, Life, July 10.

● 3 Nov 2003

Country Diary said that Loch Ashie just south of Inverness was once a fine breeding site for the rare Slovenian grebe (page 16, G2, October 30). It meant to say Slavonian grebe.

● 21 Oct 2004

The barn owl on page 9, yesterday, is a tawny owl.

● 25 Oct 2004

A photograph of a yellow wagtail on page 11, October 22, in a report about the decline of wild birds on British farmland, showed a variant found in continental Europe. Britain's yellow wagtail has a paler head than its continental cousin.

QUOTES AND MISQUOTES

● 21 Jan 1998

There was a misquotation from G M Hopkins's poem, "Spring and Fall", in a column on page 14, January 19. He did not write, "Margaret, are you grieving / Over Goldengrove unleavening?" The word he used was "unleaving".

● 22 Jan 1998

In the obituary for Ewart Abner (page 18, January 15), we mistakenly gave the title of one of his songs, recorded by the El Dorados, as "In My Front Room". This was a step too far. The song is correctly called "At My Front Door".

● 24 Mar 1999

An attempt to quote Pistol misfired at the end of an article, Good, bad and awful, page 18, yesterday. We attributed to him the "famous war cry": "Lets [sic] kill all the lawyers." The words belong to Dick, the butcher, in *Henry VI*, Part II, Act IV, Scene II: "The first thing we do, let's kill all the lawyers."

● 23 Apr 1999

A note in our arts diary, page 13, April 17, about the failure of the lights at the reopening of the Rose Theatre said " ... all we saw – like Marvel looking at God – was a deep but dazzling darkness". It was not Andrew Marvel but Henry Vaughan who saw in God "a deep, but dazzling darkness" (from Vaughan's poem "The Night").

● 27 Apr 1999

Correction to a correction, page 21, April 23: Andrew Marvell, the poet, is spelt with a double l (Captain Marvel, the comic book hero, has one).

11 Aug 1999

The "dirty British coaster" of John Masefield's poem, quoted by a columnist on Monday on page 14, has a salt-caked, not a salt-stained smokestack.

13 Aug 1999

Milton's poem on Oliver Cromwell refers to him as "our chief of men" not "our first of men", as a columnist (page 18, yesterday) had it.

3 Oct 2000

In recommending Laurence Olivier's *Henry V*, among the week's best films on television, page 53, the Guide, September 30, we drew particular attention to his "St Swithin's Day" speech before the battle of Agincourt. We called it "a heroic rabble-rouser". It was, of course, St Crispin's Day. This is how the speech, from Act IV, scene iii, concludes: "And gentlemen in England, now a-bed / Shall think themselves accurs'd they were not here,/ And hold their manhoods cheap whiles any speak/ That fought with us upon Saint Crispin's day."

7 Oct 2000

In our lead feature in G2 yesterday about cannabis, we asked people whether they smoked it and quoted the former leader of the SNP, Alex Salmond as saying: "If you say 'yes' people claim you're encouraging and supporting it and if you say 'no' it looks like you're a prick." Mr Salmond has asked us to make it clear that what he actually said was "prig", not "prick".

20 Dec 2000

A misprint of "public" in the Saturday Review, page 2, December 16, resulted in Neville Cardus being quoted of writing on Shaw: "We had been repressed so long in our pubic discussions ... an hour of it and not a fumble."

4 Nov 2002

In discussing the work of Gainsborough, pages 12 and 13, G2, October 29, our critic referred to the artist's *Diana and Actaeon*, "in which a bevvy of naked women disport themselves ..." Bevy: a group, esp of girls. Bevvy: a drink, esp an alcoholic one. "We had a few bevvies last night." Both definitions, *Collins*.

13 Jun 2001

Shakespeare went awry in a column, page 9, G2, yesterday, in which John Prescott and Ann Widdecombe were seen as "the Viola and Sebastian of politics – *Twelfth Night* twins fatefully separated at birth". In fact they were separated in a shipwreck on the shores of Illyria.

9 May 2002

In our editorial about the threat to the oak tree, page 15, May 6, we misquoted David Garrick's words to the famous song. They are not "Hearts of oak ..." etc, but "Heart of oak are our ships, heart of oak are our men ..." – a reader pointed out the correct (singular) version in a letter, page 15, May 7.

23 May 2002

Ophelia is not buried hugger-mugger, as we suggested in a piece about language, Back to basics, page 23, G2, yesterday – but her father, Polonius, is. It is the king in *Hamlet* who says of Polonius: "We have done but greenly in hugger-mugger to inter him."

10 Jul 2002

A column – page 18, July 8, Livingstone must serve his sentence – doubted that London's mayor recently persuaded the chancellor to "abandon the callous habits of a lifetime". That was a glitch in dictation: it was meant to be cautious habits of a lifetime.

29 Aug 2002

The theme song of George Formby was not, as Smallweed said, page 20, August 24, "I'm standing by the lamppost at the corner of the street". In fact, George Formby sang "I'm leaning on a lamppost at the corner of the street".

5 Sep 2002

In a report of the commemoration of Wordsworth's poem "Composed Upon Westminster Bridge", page 12, yesterday, we insinuated a Guardian apostrophe so that the view from the bridge became, "A sight so touching in it's majesty".

14 Sep 2002

A correction, page 25, September 5, was contentious. It corrected the punctuation in a line from Wordsworth's poem "Westminster Bridge", which had appeared in a report in the Guardian the previous day as: "A sight so touching in it's majesty." In fact the punctuation follows the 1807 edition and the apostrophe has been retained in all anniversary publications.

25 Sep 2002

The poet responsible for the lines quoted in the readers' editor's column, Undiluted and undeleted, page 17, September 23, was not ee cummings, but Ogden Nash: "I have a bone to pick with fate,/ Come here and tell me girly,/ Do you think my mind is maturing late,/ Or simply rotting early."

18 Nov 2002

Hugh Gaitskell, in the famous speech quoted in a panel, page 3, November 6, did not say he would fight and fight again "to save the party I love". He said: "There are some of us ... who will fight and fight and fight again to save the party we love." From a speech at the Labour conference, October 5 1960 [*Oxford Book of Quotations* online].

12 Jun 2004

Samuel Johnson said that patriotism was the last refuge of a scoundrel, not George Bernard Shaw (A cross to bear, G2, page 3, June 10).

6 Jul 2004

In our report on the first court hearing of Saddam Hussein, Leaner dictator keeps fit in jail and gives little away to captors, page 4, July 3, we managed to misquote him. Saddam did not say: "Everyone knows that Iraq is part of Kuwait." On the contrary, he said: "Everyone knows Kuwait is part of Iraq."

16 Sep 2004

We misquoted Samuel Johnson in our review of *Wodehouse: A Life* when we referred to "Johnson's famous remark about no man but a blockhead writing for money". What Boswell records Dr Johnson as saying is: "No man but a blockhead ever wrote except for money" (Plum pudding, page 9, Review, September 4).

OPEN DOOR
Glimpses of something shocking

The Readers' Editor on... questions raised by the Guardian's use of English

A reader writes from Whitstable: "For three weeks running there have been words in the Guide that I don't understand and are not in my *Concise Oxford Dictionary*. Would you please define them for me and ask the people who write this stuff to be a bit more considerate towards those of us who don't move in their circles?"

Sometimes it is better not to ask. The words were doofus, Milf, and shibbying. The editor of the Guide offers the following:

"Doofus – affectionate slang for an idiot. In fairly wide currency [in the UK], although probably American in origin.

"Milf – a term popularised in the movie *American Pie*. A teenage acronym for an attractive older woman. Mother [or Mom] I'd like to ..." Well, something beginning with f. You should have no difficulty with it if you are a regular reader of the Guardian. The editor of the Guide adds helpfully: "Now I come to think of it, there is the more polite 'yummy mummy'.

"Shibbying – stoner slang, used in the film *Dude, Where's My Car?* It means get stoned/drunk. Eg 'I shibby', 'we shibbed', 'that was some serious shibbying we did last night'. Shibby as an adjective can mean cool. 'They're a shibby band.'"

On, or near, the subject of questionable language, a reader writes from Stocksbridge on the "misuse" of the word expletive, or rather the tendency to confine it to the meaning that dictionaries give first – a swearword.

"An expletive is a purely decorative word that may be deleted without affecting meaning: hence in 'Hark! Hark! The dogs do bark', the expletive 'do' is present solely for the sake of scansion. The fact that expletives are often indelicate does not mean that an indelicate word is necessarily an expletive." I am indebted.

Another reader writes: "Given that the Guardian admirably offers corrections when it blunders, should we not expect equal attention to be given to the erroneous dissemination of incorrect linguistic information?" This reader wanted to take up discussion of the term "square meal", which had, he insisted, contrary to what we had said, nothing to do with the shape of the plate on which it was served. "Square [here] is cognate with honest, straightforward, and in the case of food, full, solid or substantial."

The English language, particularly the Guardian's use of it, is of huge fascination to readers and forms the subject of much correspondence.

Aspects that some may regard as unsavoury are not shied away from by others, but generally treated with delicacy. "'Genius-come-role model' should of course be 'cum', Latin 'with'," wrote one reader. "You may not wish to speculate on why this anglicisation is becoming increasingly common – I suspect it's because 'cum' as a misspelling of 'come' has acquired a specific sexual meaning." Which gives us a combined euphemism and homophone.

It is well to be conservative, but not too conservative. Words vary in meaning over time. Sensible concessions have to be made. A reader took exception to the use of the word "electrocute" to mean "accidental death from electric shock". He did so because it was coined, he said, in the US in the early 20th century, as a deliberate compound of "electricity" and "execute". "It refers to the death met by people sentenced to the electric chair ... Why does this disgusting word remain in (mis)use?"

The first definition in *Collins*, the Guardian's default dictionary (the dictionary to which journalists are expected to turn when a meaning or usage is not covered by the paper's own style guide) is "to kill as a result of an electric shock". The second definition, associated with the US, is "to execute in the electric chair". The style guide recognises common usage and offers this note: "electrocution – death by electric shock, so don't say survivors of torture were 'electrocuted' during their ordeal – rather that they were given electric shocks."

The report to which the reader objected concerned the death of a woman in New York by accidental electric shock. It was a perfectly appropriate word to use in the circumstances. We use it to mean any death by electric shock and not to apply only to circumstances in which someone is executed or deliberately put to death by electric shock.

Is that alright? Is alright all right? No it is not. Alright still sneaks into the Guardian. The style guide says "all right is right, alright is not all right" – a confused association with already, perhaps.

The style guide, I remind you, is a participatory thing. Feel free.

21 Feb 2004

RELIGION

Religion

● **19 Nov 1998**

In an article that posed the question, Was Jesus an architect?, Pages 10 and 11, G2, November 9, we referred to "Nazareth where Jesus was born". It is generally agreed he was born in Bethlehem.

● **5 Dec 1998**

The Immaculate Conception (Christmas Books, page 37, G2, November 27) does not describe the parthenogenetic conception of Jesus by Mary, in case we made you think it did. It is the doctrine that Mary herself was conceived by her mother without the stain of Original Sin. The Virgin Birth (*Concise Oxford*) is the doctrine of Christ's birth without a human father.

● **12 Aug 2000**

In assessing Steven Berkoff's new play, *Messiah*, an article on page 14, G2, August 10, equated the immaculate conception and Mary's impregnation. This is a recurring misconception, annually corrected in this column. The immaculate conception has nothing directly to do with the birth of Jesus. It is the doctrine that Mary herself was conceived by her mother (St Anne) without the stain of Original Sin. The Virgin Birth is the doctrine of Christ's birth without a human father.

● **7 Jan 1999**

It is the Book of Revelation (not Revelations) in the Bible. We referred to it in our report about the Concerned Christians group, Page 3, January 4.

● **6 May 1999**

In an article about Israel and the Palestinians, Peace postponed, Guardian Weekend, May 1, we referred to "worshippers of Mohammed". Muslims worship God and God alone; Mohammed is His messenger, as the Islamic creed puts it.

● **16 Jun 1999**

In the Channel Surfing column, page 4, Saturday Review, June 12, we described Balaam's ass as the ass that starved to death because it could not choose which of two equidistant bales of hay to eat. We were confusing our asses. We should have referred to Buridan's ass, from the French philosopher, Jean Buridan, who used the allegory to illustrate a particular kind of moral choice, although, as the *Encyclopaedia Britannica* points out, the animal Buridan actually mentioned was a dog, not an ass.

26 Jul 1999

In quoting the Rev Ian Paisley in our Diary, page 20, July 23, we had him warning us of a time when we would find "a prostate Christendom before the gathering forces of the EU ... " Prostrate, we meant to say.

30 Nov 1999

Sister Alessandra, the nun who has formed a band in her convent in Lombardy, page 15, November 25, was not ordained, something which does not happen to Italian nuns (it might have made her a member of the Free Churches or the Anglican Communion). When a nun joins her order permanently she is said to have solemnly professed.

15 Dec 1999

In a book review, page 9, Saturday Review, December 11, we said that "Onward Christian Soldiers" was rc (religiously correct) because it did not

mention Jesus, Mary or the Church. In fact, the second verse begins: "Like a mighty army/ Moves the Church of God"; the third verse includes the words: "But the Church of Jesus/ Constant will remain ..."; and the fourth verse: "Glory praise and honour/ Unto Christ the King!"

23 Feb 2001

Cardinal Cormac Murphy-O'Connor's new biretta became a beretta in a caption to a photograph of the papal kiss, page 14, yesterday. *Collins* allows berretta with a double r as an alternative (the Italian spelling). The Spanish spelling is birreta, one t. Beretta in the spelling we used in the caption is the name of an Italian gun manufacturer.

12 May 2001

In our Face to faith column, page 22, April 28, we said: "At the end of his life, Saint Thomas Aquinas ... came to see that faced with God, his *Summa Theologica* – and all his writings – were not straw." On the contrary, he came to see that they were straw.

14 May 2001

A feature marking the feast day of St Apollonius and warning against possible confusion with other saints similarly named, page 18, G2, April 18, was illustrated with a detail of mosaic showing St Aphthonios, who had nothing to do with the story at all.

29 May 2001

Notwithstanding the militarised state of the Holy Land at present, a reader rightly challenged our reference – Taking the tablets, Page 12, Society, May 23 – to the "Ten Commandments".

8 Feb 2002

In our report about the sale of paintings donated to the Saint Francis of Assisi Foundation, page 11, February 5, we wrongly referred to the Franciscan friars as monks, and in the heading too – Monks raise £11m from painting sale.

11 Feb 2002

In our page about pilgrimages, Resources, Key stage 2, for pupils from 7 to 11, (page 60, Education, February 5) we referred to Lourdes as a place of "medieval pilgrimage". Pilgrimages to Lourdes date only from the 19th century. Saint Bernadette, Bernadette Soubirous, was born there on January 7 1844, and saw the first apparition of the Virgin Mary in 1858.

12 Feb 2002

In our piece about William Beckford, page 5, Saturday Review, February 9, we said, "He never went to Rome ..." In fact, Beckford spent many months in Rome. What the writer had said was, "he never went over to Rome" – that is, he never converted to Catholicism.

19 Mar 2002

In Past notes, page 20, yesterday, we said, "Sadly, Descartes never had a bus company, thus robbing the world of the slogan: 'Putting the Carthusian before the horse.'" That should have been "the Cartesian before the horse". Carthusian: a member of a monastic order founded by Saint Bruno (*Collins*). Cartesian: relating to the works of Descartes.

13 Jun 2002

In the opening paragraph of Trouble in paradise, page 6, G2, June 11, we referred to "the Saint James Bible" and "the book of Peter". There is no Saint James Bible. We were thinking of the Authorised or King James Version. There is no "book of Peter" in the Bible. But there are two Letters or Epistles of (Saint) Peter in the New Testament. The quotation in the article was from The First Epistle.

18 Jul 2002

In a column, Just how many islands does Spain want?, page 5, yesterday, we referred to the Galatians as occupants of part of Spain. The Galatians, to whom Paul the Apostle addressed an Epistle, lived in central Asia Minor. It is the Galicians who occupy an autonomous region in northwest Spain.

27 Aug 2002

The clue to 4 down in our quick crossword, page 23, G2, August 22, was wrong. It suggested that Seth was the third son of Abraham. Seth was the third son of Adam and Eve (Genesis 5:3). Abraham's third son was Zimran (Genesis 25:2).

20 Sep 2002

The image of life being like the flight of a bird only briefly in the light, page 5, G2, September 18, comes from Bede's *Ecclesiastical History* (book 2, chapter 13) and not from Saint Augustine.

28 Jun 2003

A misquotation from Matthew 7:1 (King James Version) crept into a Diary item (page 20, June 26). The missing word is in brackets: "Judge not, that ye be [not] judged."

16 Aug 2003

Face to Faith, page 25, August 9, began by saying: "In a French comedy of, I think, the 16th century, there was a judge with a one-track mind, who kept asking the same question, 'Que diable allait-il faire en cette galère?' ('What the devil was he doing in that ship anyway?')." In fact, the quotation (correctly: Que diable allait-il faire dans cette galère?) is from Molière's comedy *Les Fourberies de Scapin*, and therefore 17th century. See *Brewer* (revised Igor H Evans) who says the phrase is applied to one who finds himself in difficulties through being where he ought not to be.

3 Jun 2004

A picture, page 24 (the Editor), May 26, was captioned, "Russian Orthodox nuns carry an icon during a religious procession ... in Moscow celebrating the saint's day for Cyril and Methodius, the founders of [the Cyrillic alphabet] ..." In fact, it showed two Moscow nurses carrying a Greek-inscribed icon of St Panteleimon the Great Healer, patron saint of the medical profession.

5 Mar 2001

The perils of loyalty, page 22, Comment, March 1, we referred to "the moral satin of Clinton's career". That should have read "the moral stain" etc.

5 Jul 2004

In our report, Father figure: Monumental church dedicated to controversial saint Padre Pio, page 19, July 2, we described Padre Pio as a Capuchin monk. He was a Capuchin (Franciscan) friar. See www.capuchin.com.

30 Jul 2004

An effigy of Horatio Nelson stands in Westminster Abbey and not, as we said, in Westminster Cathedral (It's all old hat, etc, page 11, yesterday). The abbey is Church of England and the cathedral, built between 1895 and 1903, is Roman Catholic.

25 Aug 2004

In a report headed Papal visit costs Lourdes £1.2m, page 17, August 19, the editing caused us to refer to "the mass read by the pontiff". Mass is "celebrated" or, in older terminology, "said".

11 Jan 2005

A reference to the United Reform Church, page 5, January 5, stopped slightly short of its correct title. It is the United Reformed Church.

12 Jan 2005

We meant to refer to Cain and Abel (The battle for Labour's soul, page 15, January 10), rather than Cain and Able.

DATES
AND TIME

● **11 Jul 1998**

In our front page story, July 9, about the copy of *The Canterbury Tales* which achieved a world record price at auction, we said it was printed by Thomas Caxton. William Caxton was the famous printer. On the Letters Page, page 25, the same day, readers leapt on an anachronism in the Austin cartoon, set in Mr Caxton's Printe Shoppe, which showed the printer saying, "Ye King says we must cut out ye Lobbyist's tale, Master Chaucer." When Caxton printed the book, Chaucer had been dead for more than 75 years.

● **20 Mar 2001**

A headline on the lead story in the Saturday Review, March 17, was stretching a point when it said that the artist Stanley Spencer visited China "just before the Cultural Revolution". Spencer visited China, as the piece said, in 1954. He died in 1959, still well before the beginning of the Cultural Revolution in 1966.

● **14 Aug 2002**

The Venetian artist Vittore Carpaccio died in 1525 or 1526 (not 1926), Portrait of the week, page 15, Review, August 10.

● **14 Aug 2002**

Antonio Vivaldi, 1678-1741 (BBC1, page 24, G2, August 12) was not a 16th-century composer.

● **18 Jan 2002**

It was wrong to refer to *The Beautiful Game* (page 5, January 16) as the West End's "first casualty of September 11". It closed on September 1.

● **14 Dec 2002**

The new film episode of Tolkien is called *The Lord of the Rings: The Two Towers*, and not *The Twin Towers*, page 14, G2, yesterday.

17 Mar 2003

The revival of interest in the music of Rebecca Clarke (Classical CDs, page 22, Friday Review, March 14) has come quicker than we suggested. She died in 1979, not 1779.

9 Jun 2003

We introduced an anachronism into our report about Lowther Castle, page 9, June 6, saying that in the 19th century the castle was visited by Boswell, Hogarth and Pitt. Boswell died in 1795, Hogarth died in 1764, William Pitt the Elder died in 1778 and William Pitt the Younger died in 1806.

11 Sep 2003

Aldo Moro was kidnapped and murdered in 1978, not 1968 as we wrongly stated in a report from the Venice film festival, page 3, September 8.

15 Apr 2004

Charles Darwin visited the Galapagos Islands in 1835 and not in 1831, as we said in this column yesterday (page 21). His voyage in the *Beagle* began in 1831.

12 Aug 2004

In a media business story, Scotsman rewinds clock by turning tabloid, page 16, August 10, we said the Scotsman was first published in 1831. In fact the Scotsman was founded as a tabloid or compact in 1817. It became a broadsheet in 1831.

20 Aug 2004

Bach's Well Tempered Clavier was not written in the early 19th century, as we said in an interview with Daniel Barenboim. It was written in 1722. Bach died in 1750 (Home entertainment, Friday Review, page 18, August 13).

20 Sep 2001

A columnist, wrote as follows on page 6, G2, yesterday: "In the Times, Michael Gove has devised the word 'Guardianistas', for the pantywaists (nervous nellies) who read this paper ..." The columnist saw in the word the imputation of effeminacy and said, "Me, I'm a Guardianisto ..." In fact, there is nothing feminine or effeminate in Spanishista endings which indicate neuter nouns as in periodista (Spanish for journalist).

● **27 Sep 2004**

In a review of the film, *The Ister*, page 18, the Friday Review, September 24, we said the title came from a work by the 17th-century German poet Hölderlin. In fact, Hölderlin's dates are 1770-1843, placing him in the 18th and 19th centuries.

● **29 Sep 2004**

Sid Vicious lived from 1957 to 1979, not from 1957 to 1959 as we said in a panel accompanying a report about the new *Dictionary of National Biography* (Pytheas, Diana, the singing postman, page 3, September 23).

● **1 Oct 2004**

We were wrong to say in a column (page 9, yesterday) that the late Sir David English "was charmed to be introduced to baby Leo Blair". Sir David died in 1998 and Leo Blair was born two years later in 2000. We meant to refer to Sir David's successor as editor of the Daily Mail, Paul Dacre.

● **19 Oct 2004**

A caption, Miles Davies at Ronnie [Scott]'s in 2001, page 15, Arts, G2, yesterday, was in error. Miles Davis (not Davies) died in 1991.

OPEN DOOR
A rule without reason

The Readers' Editor on... the long struggle between "alright" and "all right"

At the end of my last column on the Guardian's use of English, I commented on the alright/ all right controversy, quoting the Guardian style guide: "All right is right, alright is not all right" – and I suggested that the "alright" form may have arisen from confusion with already (which is all right).

There was an immediate flurry of correspondence from readers anxious to speak up for "alright". One reader wrote: "I have been innocently using alright for years as in 'Are you hurt? – No, I'm alright.' I looked in my *Chambers Dictionary*, which told me that alright was an alternative, less acceptable spelling of all right.

"I would, of course, use all right as in 'today his sums were all right,' where the meaning seems to me to be entirely different." On the comparison with "already", the reader suggests: "This would seem to be a good model for alright. 'We are all ready' has a completely different meaning from 'She already knows'."

This reader ended with a plea: "It is well recognised that the language is constantly changing, and some of us resist some of these changes fiercely, often with strong backing from the Guardian. However, I intend to go on using alright as I have done in the past, and it would make me really happy if the Guardian were to tell me that it was all right."

Let us get the disappointment out of the way immediately. The Guardian, which has been revising its style guide, since published in book form, has every intention of sticking to the definition with which this column opened: all right is right, alright is not all right.

The 1933 edition of the *Oxford English Dictionary* described the word "alright" as obsolete, having meant "just, exactly". It quoted only two examples, one from c1175 and the other from c1230. By the time of the 1972 supplement, the dictionary was at least prepared to concede the reappearance of the word as "a frequent spelling of all right". Its earliest quoted example was from the *Durham University Journal*, 1893: "I think I shall pass alright." This quotation highlights a distinction of meaning that a colleague, agreeing with my correspondent, believes might be usefully served by preserving "alright": "Your examination answers do not have to be all right for the result to be alright." Others to whom "alright" is an abhorrence argue that even in such a sentence as that the context makes the distinction in meaning apparent: "Your examination results do not have to be all right for the result to be all right."

The 1972 supplement to the *OED* concludes with a quotation from the first edition (1926) of HW Fowler's *Modern English Usage*: "There are no such forms as all-right, allright or alright, though even the last, if seldom allowed by compositors to appear in print, is often seen ... [in manuscript]."

A more recent edition of Fowler, the *New Modern English Usage*, revised third edition, edited by RW Burchfield (Oxford 1998) reserves one of its snootier notes for the subject: "The use of 'all right', or inability to see that there is anything wrong with 'alright', reveals one's background, upbringing, education etc, perhaps as much as any word in the language ... It is preferred, to judge from the evidence I have assembled, by popular sources like the British magazines *The Face*, the *New Musical Express* ... the *Socialist Worker* ... and hardly ever by writers of standing." Quoted exceptions are Chinua Achebe, 1987: "You'll be alright, love" and Anita Desai, 1988: "'Yes, they visit tombs and live in ashrams alright,' Farrokh sneered."

Within the Guardian, despite its own rule, "alright" has a persistent presence, with almost 700 examples coming up in an electronic search from the past year or two. Figuring prominently among the users of "alright" is Guardian Unlimited, particularly in sport and popular music: "Great entertainment and the cricket's alright as well"; "It's sensational stuff, alright!" But it crops up in other areas too: "I read it alright and I know it's got your name on it, but who wrote it?" (Review).

Kingsley Amis, in *The King's English* (HarperCollins 1997), wrote: "I still feel that to inscribe 'alright' is gross, crass, coarse and to be avoided, and I say so now." But why it is all those things no one seems to know.

Kingsley Amis again: "Its interdiction is as pure an example as possible of a rule without a reason, and in my case may well show nothing but how tenacious a hold early training can take." In the Guardian's case, consistency is the elusive object.

27 Mar 2004

IDENTITY

16 Feb 1999

The Endpiece column (Page 14, yesterday) was wrong to say that Danton was stabbed to death in his bath. He wasn't: he was guillotined. It was Marat who was stabbed in the bath.

10 Mar 1999

In a column on page 16, March 8, we said of Gordon Brown that we were certain he subscribed to "all those Victorian saws with which Ford Maddox Ford surrounded his most famous painting. 'Seest thou a man diligent in his business? He shall stand before Kings.'" Ford Madox (one d) Ford, 1873-1939, was a writer. Ford Madox (one d) Brown was the painter of *Work* in Manchester City Art Gallery, the person and the painting to which we meant to refer. His painting *The Last Of England*, in Birmingham City Art Gallery, is also often claimed as his most famous painting.

29 Mar 1999

In an obituary of Kirk Alyn, who played Superman, we referred to the character as the "Caped Crusader". That was Batman, not Superman.

13 Oct 1999

In one of our editions yesterday the poem "Cost of Life", was attributed to Andrew Morton, "the poet laureate", a title held by the real author of the piece, Andrew Motion. Andrew Morton is the biographer of Princess Diana and Monica Lewinsky. The "ass-mess" in the "Morton" version should have been "ash-mess". Apologies to both.

11 Nov 1999

The two giant cranes at Harland and Wolff which dominate the Belfast shipyard are nicknamed Samson and Goliath, not Samson and Delilah as given in an article on the company (page 11, yesterday).

8 Mar 2000

In early editions of an article headed, I'm backing the Pope, page 22, yesterday, we began, "Pope John XXIII is very active ..." Quite the contrary, of course, since he died in 1963. We corrected that in later editions to "Pope John Paul II ..." Pope John Paul II has appointed two archbishops in England and Wales recently, Cormac Murphy-O'Connor to Westminster and Vincent Nichols to Birmingham.

13 Nov 2000

In our account of Lou Kenton's experiences in the Spanish civil war, page 2, G2, November 10, there was a sentence starting, "When Khruschev's tanks rolled into Prague ..." They were Brezhnev's tanks.

10 Oct 2001

In an article headed They came in search of paradise, page 14, G2, October 8, we said that the film star Robert Donat was a Hungarian. He was born in Withington, Manchester, in 1905. His father was Polish.

2 Sep 2002

The image captioned "Charles I", page 20, G2, August 30, in fact shows Oliver Cromwell.

16 Aug 2002

Arundhati Roy was cast for a short period in an article in MediaGuardian.co.uk as a "well-known British Asian". Her Indian nationality has now been restored.

12 Dec 2002

In a report, No one "nudged" us – Home Office, page 4, yesterday, we referred to the Home Office minister as Beverley Knight. Beverley Knight is a soul singer. The Home Office minister for immigration and asylum is Beverly Hughes.

7 Feb 2003

In a piece about lesbianism, Girls, uninterrupted, pages 14 and 15, G2, yesterday, we said "Madonna, on the other hand, was quite happy to encourage rumours that she was having an affair with the actress Sarah Bernhardt". That would be Sandra Bernhard, rather than the Divine Sarah. In the same piece kd laing should have been kd lang.

21 Mar 2003

In a report, Thriving rural railways forgive Beeching at last, page 14, March 19, we referred to the entertainers Donald Flanders and Michael Swann. We meant to say Michael Flanders and Donald Swann.

5 Jul 2003

In a tennis report, page 29, July 2, we said Henman rather resembled Richard Hannay in "Albert Hitchcock's classical [sic] version of ... *The Thirty-Nine Steps*". Alfred Hitchcock we meant.

10 Sep 2003

Nicholas Soames was accidentally knighted in our report headed Bourgeois image haunts National Trust (page 11, September 6).

14 Oct 2003

We said yesterday that Michael Crick is the son of political philosopher Bernard Crick (Formidable reporter whose name strikes fear, page 4). Sir Bernard wishes us to point out that this is not so. As does Pat Crick, Michael's mother, who assures us that his father is John Crick, a retired FE lecturer.

6 Nov 2003

An editing error turned the dancer and choreographer Inbal Pinto into a man (Reviews, page 22, November 3). She is a woman.

12 Nov 2003

A picture purporting to show the film director Sam Peckinpah in yesterday's prize quiz was actually of the late actor James Mason (page 23, G2).

18 Nov 2003

The photograph purporting to be Alan Bates in the prize quiz yesterday, G2, page 23, was of his colleague and contemporary, Tom Courtenay.

19 Nov 2003

Hendrix lived in the same Mayfair street as Handel, not Haydn, as was said in the prize quiz, G2, page 23, yesterday.

14 Jan 2004

We had the two figures in a photograph, page 14, yesterday, the wrong way round. Prince Juan Carlos was on the left, not the right. He was shown doing karate exercises with King Constantine II of Greece.

3 Mar 2004

In reviewing the Channel 4 programme *Bodyshock: The Man Who Ate His Lover*, page 22, G2, yesterday, we confused the eater with the eaten at one point. To be clear about it, the person eating was Armin (Meiwes), and the person eaten was Bernd (Jurgen Brandes).

16 Apr 2004

Julius Caesar, not Caeser (twice in Pick of the Day, G2, page 24, April 12).

21 Jun 2004

The Belgian philosopher who lends his name to a building in Brussels (Beachhead for Ukip etc, page 13, June 18) is, as it correctly said on first mention in the text, Justus Lipsius (1547-1606). It was his misfortune to become Lustis Jipsius, later in the same story.

21 Jun 2004

The Swiss coach's name is Köbi Kuhn, not Kobi Kühn (Curfew shame still haunts Kuhn [sic], page 7, Sport, June 16).

4 Aug 2004

George W Bush was born in Connecticut and educated in a Massachusetts boarding school and then at Yale University, also in Connecticut. So we were a little wide of the mark in claiming he is "a Texan, born and brought up in America's oil state" (Oil and troubled waters, Review, page 7, July 31). Texas can claim two native-born presidents, Dwight Eisenhower and Lyndon Johnson.

27 Feb 2004

The "soldiers" shown in silhouette on the *Ark Royal* in the picture on page 6, yesterday, are sailors.

10 Aug 2004

It is Humphrey Lyttelton, not Lyttleton (page 20, G2, August 6).

7 Jan 2005

We mistakenly said that Einstein was "a 26-year-old postal clerk [when] he came up with his special theory of relativity" (Relativity for dummies, G2 page 4, January 6). He was employed in the Swiss patent office, not the post office.

OPEN DOOR
Life without the asterisk

The Readers' Editor on... **offensive language and the Guardian's guidelines**

Two stories on the front page of the Guardian on successive days last month in which unexpurgated expletives were used, once again focused attention on the paper's policy on offensive language. One story involved the language and behaviour of the owner of the Daily Express, Richard Desmond, at a meeting with executives of the Daily Telegraph. The other was concerned with racist comments which led to the resignation from ITV of Ron Atkinson and the curtailment of his work for the sports pages of the Guardian.

In both stories the offending words were spelt out. One reader called on the day the Desmond story was published to register his strong objection to the use of the word "fuck" in the story and to say he was cancelling his Guardian.

Both of these stories, in fact, fell within the Guardian guidelines and the publication of the spoken expletives in both cases was in my view justified.

This is not so with some of the occurrences which now appear in clear breach of the guidelines and which often attract complaint. One journalist said the proliferation of the words in the Guardian sometimes reminded him of the Flanders and Swann song: "Ma's out, Pa's out, let's talk rude! Pee Po Belly Bum Drawers ..."

In the past year the word "fuck" appeared in 722 stories in the Guardian, divided almost equally between the main broadsheet part of the paper and its supplements. The word "cunt" – to which many of the paper's own journalists as well as readers take strong exception – appeared in about 70 stories.

The editor's guidelines say: "Remember the reader – respect demands that we should not casually use words that are likely to offend. Use such words only when absolutely necessary to the facts of a piece, or to portray a character in an article; there is almost never a case in which we need to use a swearword outside direct quotes. The stronger the swearword, the harder we ought to think about using it. Never use asterisks, which are just a cop-out." There is also a caution against the use of swearwords in headings.

I sought the opinion of Guardian journalists with the following email: "It is pretty clear that the guidance in the style guide is being widely ignored. The f-word is three times more likely to be encountered in the Guardian than in the Independent, the c-word is four times more likely to be met in the Guardian than the Independent. The words hardly ever or never occur in the other papers, broadsheet or tabloid. Is the Guardian's attitude OK? Too slack? Or should any attempt at control be abandoned (should the guidelines be scrapped?). Is the Guardian right to spell the words out? Or should it revert to the common convention of asterisks as in f***?"

About 100 journalists replied, of whom only 10 favoured the use of asterisks. One said: "For some parents with young families, those trying to teach their kids about appropriate language and behaviour, it presents a problem: a paper they like and respect becomes the equivalent of a person they're wary of letting into the house, one who might use foul language in front of the kids."

The overwhelming opinion, however, was strongly against the use of asterisks. "Fuck is one of the commonest words in British demotic speech. Asterisks are silly and genteel and merely make the paper look fussy – they are the equivalent of Hyacinth Bucket." About half of the respondents to my email said the use of asterisks would be retrograde, patronising and coy. One said: "The paper should reflect the way people use language in the real world."

The editor of the Guide, which regularly attracts complaints, said: "When I started editing in 2000, I was amazed at the coarse language people use quite casually in copy ... Now I find myself, with a roster of youngish writers covering popular culture, trying to negotiate some sort of taste line that allows for funny, frank and unfusty writing without being gratuitously offensive. I'm not sure you can get a uniform tone that pleases every age and social group – unless you just go for neutral with a blanket ban."

No one wants that. A couple of people believed the guidelines should be abandoned because they were plainly not working and the whole thing should be left to the discretion of individual section editors.

Some thought the guidelines should be more stringent. More than half the journalists thought the guidelines were good and would still allow the paper to recognise changes in society if they were more vigorously applied. That is my view too.

8 May 2004

NATIONALITY and FOREIGN LANGUAGE

● 16 Feb 1998

A review of the BBC1 programme, *Pleasure Beach*, Page 19, G2, February 10, expressed some puzzlement about the connection between a young Spanish woman and escudos. She wasn't Spanish. She was Portuguese, like the escudos.

● 17 Oct 1998

In a letter on page 20, October 10, we said that the Finnish word for dyslexia (reading disturbance) was lukihiri. The writer of the letter has been in touch to say this was our misprint. The word she wanted us to use was lukihäiriö. Apologies.

● 9 Nov 1998

The superb French soprano mentioned in Buried pleasures, page 25, Friday Review, is Belgian (b Brussels 1911).

● 29 Sep 2000

Danish department: from Pass Notes on Denmark, page 3, G2, yesterday, where we said we had "a whole smorrebrod of alternative dodgy cultural references". Dodgy indeed. Smörrebröd is the Danish for sandwich. We probably meant smörgåsbord, which is not Danish, but Swedish for sandwich-table or buffet.

● 9 Jun 2003

The multilingual countdown at the head of a column, Mars in their eyes, page 23, June 6, was perhaps not quite as intended: "Cinque ... fünf ... trés ... two ... un! Nous avons eine lift-off!" It begins with two fives (in Italian and German). Four in German would be vier. Tres, if it is Spanish, has no accent.

19 Jan 2000

In a panel about correction fluid, page 3, Office hours, January 17, we said, "Fed up with having to rip up pages after her all-too-frequent typing slips, she simply hid the evidence with a blob of white tempura paint ..." Tempera, that would be.

24 Jun 2003

Roman Polanski became a Czech in the Guide, page 8, June 21. He is Polish.

10 Jul 2003

It is Wilhelm Furtwängler (not Fürtwängler), Liebestod, not Liebstod, and Der (not Die) Fliegende Holländer, page 20, Friday Review, July 4.

12 Jun 2004

A football match between Denmark and Sweden cannot be likened to A-Ha versus Abba, as we did in a profile of the Danish team, page 48 of the Euro 2004 guide issued with the Guardian, June 7. A-Ha is a Norwegian band.

18 Jun 2004

A profile of the Slovak tennis player Daniela Hantuchova was accompanied by the flag of the Czech Republic, instead of the Slovak flag (Wimbledon 2004 guide, page 59, yesterday).

19 Aug 2004

In one of the notes in Pick of the day, page 21, G2, yesterday, we appeared to attach the term British to the football team of the Republic of Ireland, which was included in a list with Wales and Scotland. Sorry.

23 Sep 2004

In our report of the record run of the tilting train, the pendolino (page 6, September 21), we translated its name from the Italian as "she who leans". Pendolino (a masculine noun) means, among other things, pendulum, something that goes one way and another without going too far.

5 Oct 2004

It is *le coeur*, not *la coeur*, Diary, page 15, October 2.

10 Nov 2004

Bangalore is not India's "silicone valley", a caption, page 24, November 8. As the Guardian stylebook puts it: "silicon, computer chips; silicone, breast implants".

MISSPELLING

8 Apr 1998
A letter, Page 17, March 31, complimenting Mr Blair on his use of French, misspelt *merveilleuse*.

8 Apr 1998
A short item on the Simpsons in Florence, Page 21, Friday Review, January 8, contained a number of errors including the following: it referred to hoards of tourists (instead of hordes); Siena appeared in its archaic anglicised form (with a double n); the Palazzo Pitti came out as the Palazzo Pizzi; the Boboli Gardens became Bolotti; the Ponte Vecchio became the Ponte de Vecchio; the Uffizi Gallery was misspelt and was said to be the home of Michelangelo's David. David is in the Accademia.

17 Feb 2001
Small point from an article about race and The Archers, page 6, G2, yesterday, xenophobia is spelt with an x not a z.

19 Apr 2001
The dolphins did not talk (Net deaths put species at risk, page 11, April 14) in spite of the impression given by our caption, which said that bottlenose dolphins were "in urgent need of conversation measures". It is conservation that is needed, particularly in the Moray Firth, which we incorrectly called the Murray Firth.

15 May 2001
Pharaoh, a word commonly misspelt – as pharoah – appeared wrongly again in a heading and caption on page 7, yesterday (a report headed Pyramids seen as stairways to heaven). It was correct in the report itself. A reader suggests "arse over head" as a useful mnemonic.

19 Jun 2001
From page 5, Media, yesterday: "those [journalists] who went there [the Westminster lobby] via public school and Oxbridge remain under the delusion that all architecture is gothic, all deserts are served with custard ..." "Desserts" that would be.

24 Nov 2001

The writer of a column about misspelling, including his own inability to spell, page 5, G2, yesterday, sympathised with Dan Quayle's "infamous" gaffe in adding an e to tomato. He did not. He added an e to potato (potatoe).

16 Jan 2002

The former heroine addict, page 4, Office Hours, January 14, was a former heroin addict.

17 Apr 2002

The Miles Davis album referred to in Pills and thrills (Friday Review, page 2, April 12), is *Sketches of Spain*, not *Sketches of Pain*.

21 Sep 2002

We meant to describe Martin Stephen as the high master of Manchester Grammar (rather than Grammer) School, page 18, yesterday.

30 Oct 2004

From Society, page 13, October 27: "Your wallet can be a powerful weapon in the war against equality." Inequality, we should have said.

10 Oct 2002

The reference in a letter, about the prison diaries of Jeffrey Archer, to "publish and be dammed" should, of course, have been to "publish and be damned" [we think].

28 Nov 2002

In an item, Spelling department, page 5, G2, yesterday, we misspelt synecdoche (we said synedoche). We also defined the word wrongly, saying that it described a figure of speech where part of a word stood for the whole. In fact it is where (*Collins*) a part is substituted for a whole, or a whole for a part, eg, 50 head of cattle, a fleet of sail.

17 Dec 2002

A letter printed under the general heading, No rush to sign up for the boycott (page 23, December 13) asked, "why hasn't this self-evident truth peculated into the blind righteousness of the boycott organisers?" Percolated was the word required. To peculate is to appropriate or embezzle public money (*Collins*).

22 Nov 2003

Our apology (Corrections, page 27, November 19) for innacuracies, requires an apology. We meant inaccuracies.

21 Jan 2004

Monday's quick crossword, page 23, G2, required the answer to 2 Down to be misspelt "millenia", instead of "millennia". Many readers were reluctant to do that.

24 Jan 2004

Ghandi makes its appearance with depressing regularity in our pages where the misspelling appears more frequently than in most other papers. Mahatma Gandhi is the correct spelling (review of Joan Baez at the Philharmonic Hall, Liverpool, page 20, January 19).

26 Jan 2004

There is no such word as restauranteur, despite its appearance in a television preview, page 17, G2, January 23.

10 Mar 2004

The title of the Irish prime minister, taoiseach, was spelled incorrectly throughout an article headlined, Scandal that could dent the Teflon taioseach (sic), page 10, March 6. A misspelling in the Guardian style guide has now been corrected.

2 Jul 2004

In a brief item, Beckham marked, page 6, June 30, we said that a photographic portrait of David Beckham on view at the Royal Academy of Arts in London had been inscribed with "You losers". In fact, it was inscribed: "You loosers".

11 Dec 2004

The "grizzly find" in the Thames, a caption, page 4, G2, yesterday, was, in fact, grisly.

18 Dec 2004

Parkhurst maximum security prison in the Isle of Wight became Pankhurst prison for the duration of one edition, Colonel's secret past is novel twist etc, page 10, yesterday.

GRAMMAR

Grammar

14 Dec 1999

English department: from a television review, page 18, December 10: "The victim lays on the ground, sobbing." That should be "The victim lies on the ground," or if the past tense is wanted, "The victim lay on the ground". See the notes on usage for lay, *Collins Millennium*.

21 Feb 2000

An unwanted hyphen changed the meaning of the following passage in our review of the film *Topsy-Turvy*, page 8, Friday Review, February 18: "... when Gilbert and his wife visited a Japanese exhibition, which is shown as inspiring the *Mikado*, his wife claims to have seen three-minute Japanese ladies there ..." We meant to say small rather than brief.

9 Aug 2000

One more hyphen perhaps in the following, from our report about the day it rained sprats in Great Yarmouth, page 2, August 7: "The two inch-long sprats covered a garden shed and several lawns in the area ..."

12 Dec 2000

The lower-case christmas in our note about the Top 10 cookbooks, page 11, Saturday Review, December 9, was just a slip. Christmas still has an initial capital, even in the Guardian.

22 Jul 2002

English department: from page 3, July 19: "The academic – whom authorities have long believed was connected to the group ... – was seized on Wednesday ..." That should be who, not whom.

24 Jul 2002

A headline, One in 20 women have been raped (page 2, yesterday), should have said "has". The same error was made in the first paragraph of the article.

3 Sep 2002

In a table entitled Excessive vitamin intake, which accompanied the article, Watchdogs to set limits on vitamin intake (page 7, August 30), it was said that boron "might effect reproduction". No such miracle supplement is yet on the market. "Affect" was the intended word.

17 Feb 2003

In our piece about Frida Kahlo, pages 2 to 4, Friday review, February 14, an unwanted comma replaced a necessary hyphen to produce the following, "the legendary gangster, movie star and sensitive art collector Edward G Robinson ..." We meant to call him a "gangster-movie star".

2 Apr 2003

From page 22, March 29: "But this week another scenario hoved into view." Hove is a past tense and past participle of heave. There is no hoved.

12 May 2003

St Andrews University referred to in the obituary of Berkeley Smith, page 19, May 6, does not sport the apostrophe imposed on it in the editing. The town of the same name does not have one either.

14 Aug 2003

Our preview note for the television programme, *That'll Teach 'Em*, in which a group of 16-year-olds experience 1950s-style education, page 24, G2, August 12, contained the following: "... the pupils ... get to grips with past particles, syntax and grammar." Past participles are what they struggled with in those days.

20 Aug 2003

An editing error in the opening paragraph of an article headlined Poisoned chalice, about the International Monetary Fund (Comment, page 19), yesterday, obscured the sense intended. The writer was accusing the IMF of engineering disaster, not of being "an engineering disaster".

17 Jan 2005

The plague of the apostrofly, from page 24, Life, January 13: "Mobile's aren't always welcome."

20 Jan 2005

The apostrofly strikes again: "Saturday's are the worst ..." (Half empty, G2, page 23, January 17).

ENGLISH

31 Mar 2000

English department: from a column, page 21, March 29, in which we referred to "... the missionary position that produced sexual misery for millions of white, western women, rendered prone and very, very sad". Missionary position: a position for sexual intercourse in which the man lies on top of the woman and they are face to face. Prone: lying flat or face downwards. Supine: lying or resting on the back with the face upwards (all definitions, *Collins*).

9 May 2000

We said in a book review, page 9, Saturday Review, May 6, that "Darwin was particularly troubled by the peacock whose exuberant tail appeared to flaunt the logic of natural selection". We meant to say that in flaunting its tail it appeared to flout the rules.

7 Jun 2000

The writer of a letter (Don Mathew), page 19, yesterday, wanted to say that his transport proposals were "child-friendly" and would address "social exclusion issues". This, strangely, became "coal exclusion issues". Sorry.

13 Jul 2000

From a parliamentary sketch, page 2, July 11, where we referred to "a joke which in any comedy club would have evinced whistles ..." Evoked (a word commonly confused with evince).

28 Jul 2000

From our television notes, page 24, G2, yesterday: "When it comes to adopting a baby in the US, there's only really one criteria – money." You can have any number of criteria except one.

24 Aug 2000

A heading for Inside Story, G2, page 4, yesterday, referred to "Hollywood's only publically acknowledged lesbian couple". The word is publicly. In the same edition's broadsheet, page 2, two-minute Guardian flagged our inquiry into "boardroom renumeration". Remuneration, that is.

● **15 Sep 2000**

From a column on page 9, Parents, G2, September 13: "… as if I were any more likely to use this ridiculous fop to world environmental destruction the second time around." Fop: A man who is excessively concerned with fashion and elegance (*Collins*). Sop: a bribe or concession etc, given to placate or mollify (same source). To give a sop to Cerberus (the three-headed dog at the gates of Hades) "When persons died the Greeks and Romans used to put a cake in their hands as a sop to Cerberus to allow them to pass without molestation." (*Brewer's Dictionary of Phrase & Fable*).

● **18 Sep 2000**

From a piece about the television programme *Big Brother*, page 2, G2, September 15: "[She] kept demanding that the evictees ditch the dirt on events in the house." You can ditch a boyfriend or girlfriend, but you dish the dirt ("spread malicious gossip" *Collins*).

● **19 Sep 2000**

From page 8, Weekend, September 16, where we said, "The higher you hoist your petard, the more unequivocal its salute …", perhaps confusing petard with pennant. The writer is making a distant reference to

Shakespeare: *Hamlet*, III, iv, "… For 'tis sport to have the engineer/ Hoist with his own petard …" *Brewer's Dictionary of Phrase & Fable* defines it thus: "Beaten with his own weapons, caught in his own trap," and tells us, "The petard was a thick iron engine of war, filled with gunpowder, and fastened to gates, barricades, etc, to blow them up. The danger was lest the engineer who fired the petard should be blown up [into the air = hoist, *OED*] by the explosion." Petard, probably from the French, peter, break wind.

● **26 Oct 2000**

In our obituary of Eduard Goldstücker, page 24, yesterday, we said, "He passionately opposed the distortion of truth and the fortification of history". Falsification, that should have been. Our mistake.

● **30 Nov 2000**

In our obituary of Conrad Voss Bark, whom we described as a journalist and fly-fishing enthusiast, page 24, yesterday, we said his pastimes included typing files. He much preferred tying flies, of course. The obituarist is exonerated.

● 1 Feb 2001

In a radio review, page 20, G2, January 29, we said, confusingly: "A widower told of the treatment her husband had received ..."

● 24 Mar 2001

The reader who promised a deferential touch of her fetlock, Letters, page 21, yesterday, would probably be touching, or tugging, her forelock.

● 10 Apr 2001

In an obituary of John Ardoin, the music critic, page 20, yesterday, we said the most important of his four books on Maria Callas, *The Callas Legacy*, "analysed all her recordings in scrumptious detail". We meant to say "scrupulous detail".

● 23 May 2001

An After hours item on the benefits of tango dancing (Page 16, Office Hours, May 21) said: "Once you are proficient, wardrobe is of tantamount importance." That would be paramount.

● 23 May 2001

Our obituary on page 24 yesterday of Sam Sherry, acrobatic dancer, clog dancer and singer, said: "His slight fame always belied the energy and excitement of his dancing." The intention was, frame.

● 26 Nov 2001

In a review of a Pulp concert, page 16, November 20, we referred to the "moribund dry wit" of Jarvis Cocker. We meant to say mordant. (Moribund: near death, without force or vitality; mordant: sarcastic, caustic, pungent – *Collins*).

● 25 Jan 2002

In our piece about "fossil meteorites", page 10, Science, Online, yesterday, we said: "One meteorite reputably sits directly on top of a trilobite fossil ..." We meant to say "reputedly sits" etc.

● 2 Jul 2002

An unnoticed error in a letter to the editor, page 19, yesterday, allowed the writer to say of the once disparaged holdings of "French peasants", "Such small mixed farms are now naturally praised as the organic ordeal." Ideal, that would be.

● 9 Sep 2002

A column, Bomb the lot of them, page 17, September 6, began: "I love this time of year – the climactic anomalies of summer drift imperceptibly into the climactic anomalies of autumn ..." The writer meant to say climatic.

● **19 Nov 2002**

An editing slip introduced a bizarre proposal for a legislative measure in the Queen's speech (Tories and Lib Dems home in on civil rights, page 12, November 13) when we said: "Parents of persistent truants are likely to be made subject to patenting orders, rather than fines." That should, of course, have been "parenting orders".

● **20 Dec 2002**

In a leader, Transport slowdown, page 19, December 18, we said, "The centrality of the car in everyday life cannot be underestimated." We meant to say overestimated.

● **20 Nov 2002**

In our note on the UN's primary education for all programme, page 3, Education, yesterday, we said one of the targets called for "the halving of literacy rates". We meant to say "illiteracy rates".

● **1 Apr 2003**

Common English errors 1 (from Business notebook, page 24, March 28): "If he's right, the criticisms ... could rapidly rise to a crescendo." Crescendo is the rising, and what is risen to is a climax.

Common English errors 2 (from page 18, some editions of G2, yesterday): "[David Hare's *Racing Demons*] hones in on a single aspect of contemporary British life." It homes in.

● **6 May 2003**

When we referred to "Anger over the Iraq war and dissolution with the first terms of the Scottish parliament" (Subdued success for Labour, page 12, May 2) we meant to say disillusion rather than dissolution.

● **15 Aug 2003**

The "coruscating" letter to the BBC from Alastair Campbell, Hutton Inquiry sketch, page 5, August 13, should have been "excoriating". Coruscating: emitting flashes of light, sparkling. Excoriating: denouncing vehemently, censuring severely (*Collins*).

● **15 Nov 2003**

In describing the sexual activity of the main character in the new film *The Mother* as including "torpid afternoons in bed with her daughter's boyfriend", we reversed the entire meaning of the article (torpid: apathetic, sluggish or lethargic). Torrid – highly charged emotionally – was the word required (Why make do with cocoa?, G2, page 14, November 13).

● **24 Nov 2003**

Saul Bellow was an expatriate living in Paris, not an ex-patriot as we said in After the flood, Review, page 4, November 15.

● **16 Mar 2004**

We meant to say that Bob Marley's posthumous albums were flawed, not "floored" (Stop this obscenity, Friday Review, page 4, March 12).

● **19 Mar 2004**

We described a documentary on Isambard Kingdom Brunel, Men of Iron, as being "enervating" when, from the context of the preview, the opposite was intended (Monday, Watch this, Guide, page 68, February 21). Enervate: to deprive of strength or vitality, weaken physically or mentally debilitate (*Collins*).

● **4 Jun 2004**

In a column about the misuse of English (Amo, amas, I love a lass ..., page 21, June 2), we meant to say that fewer than 12,000 pupils were learning Latin in 2000, instead of misusing the English language by saying less than 12,000 pupils.

● **9 Jun 2004**

In a leading article about the transit of Venus, page 21, yesterday, we said: "Anyone looking today at the tiny speck that Venus is ... can get some glimpse of the enormity of the sun itself." The Guardian style guide puts it succinctly: "enormity – something monstrous or wicked, not synonymous with large."

● **23 Jul 2004**

The hint in Labour unveils reform plan, page 6, July 21, that frontbench peers might be "renumerated" was meant to suggest that they be "remunerated".

● **24 Sep 2004**

In a sentence commenting on the eventual end of Ceefax in its current form, page 2, G2, September 22, we said: "Gone will be ... the crappy pixillated graphics, the ... 'wrong' inverted comas ..." That is pixelated, and they are commas rather than comas. Pixillated means whimsical, bewildered or drunk.

● **9 Dec 2004**

The judge said to have admitted falling asleep during a trial, page 6, G2, December 6, may have been somnolent. He was certainly not somnambulant. Somnolent: drowsy, sleepy; somnambulant: walking while asleep.

FINANCE

7 Feb 2001

From a report, page 24, Finance, February 3: "He trained as a dentist for two years but gave up to join Littlewoods as a stock controller in charge of ankle stocks."

24 Jul 2001

In an article, Don't worry, mate, it's on expenses, page 10, Work, G2, July 10, we referred to the "US-owned Dresdner Kleinwort Wasserstein". It is, of course, a European bank.

31 Jul 2001

A misprint, from page 21, Jobs & Money, July 28: "... Railtrack was able to embark on a viscous circle of underinvestment leading to delays and train collisions ..."

31 Oct 2001

In an agency report, £25m plot to "blackmail" Barclays, early editions page 2, later editions page 10, yesterday, we said: "He was head of the inscription team ... responsible for devising code patterns for bank cards." That would be encryption.

11 Dec 2003

In a report, Money no longer talks in Mugabe's empire, page 15, December 9, we said that certain features of life in Harare would be familiar to "survivors of the Weiner republic". The reference was to the Weimar republic (1919 to 1933).

24 Sep 2004

The graphic that accompanied an article on tax havens and offshore financial centres, Havens that have become a tax on the world's poor, page 14, September 21, mistakenly included New Zealand.

26 May 2004

A piece about discrimination experienced by people over the age of 54, Jobs & Money, page 24, May 22, carried the headline, Wrinklies forced into the direct approach, appearing to reinforce the prejudice the text was addressing.

FLIPPING PICTURES

● **27 Jan 1998**

An archive photograph (of the Chicago Symphony Orchestra in 1978) used to illustrate an article on Page 9, G2, January 20, was printed the wrong way round, thus showing an orchestra apparently made up entirely of left-handed musicians. It was originally issued in that reversed order by Decca.

● **9 Apr 1998**

The picture of the Horsehead nebula on our front page yesterday, was reversed. To obtain the view of the nebula that we showed, the camera would need to be more than 1,500 light years away from earth.

● **7 Sep 1998**

A portrait of Lord Kitchener, reproduced on Page 10, September 4, was flipped, thus placing his medals on the wrong breast.

● **2 Oct 1998**

The great crested newt shown on the front of the Society section, September 30, was, as sober inspection confirms, upside down.

● **2 Sep 1999**

The Guardi painting of St Mark's Square, Venice, page 3, yesterday, was flipped, placing the campanile on the wrong side of the piazza. That was how it was transmitted to us and we failed to notice, unlike many readers. The original painting is in the National Gallery of Scotland in Edinburgh.

● **24 Jan 2000**

The detail of a JS Bach manuscript printed on page 13, January 11, was upside down (unlike the fragment of manuscript he was shown holding in a portrait reproduced, page 15, Friday Review, December 17. That was flipped, presenting a mirror image).

29 Feb 2000

The Salvador Dali *Christ of St John of the Cross* (Glasgow Museums), reproduced in a trail, page 15, G2, yesterday, was upside down.

1 May 2001

More than a few readers noticed that the shipwrecked people on *The Raft of the Medusa*. the painting by Gericault, page 9, Saturday Review, April 28, were sailing in the wrong direction. The picture, the original of which is in the Louvre, was accidentally reversed.

22 May 2002

The picture of the Queen, page 5, G2, yesterday, used with comments about the quality of her verse, was flipped (making her appear to be left-handed). The Guardian has a policy not to reverse or otherwise tamper with photographic images.

11 Dec 2004

We printed a black and white photograph of St Paul's Cathedral, taken in about 1950, in which the clock appears in the left tower of the west front instead of the right one. The original photograph, supplied to us by an agency, had been flipped (Pauline conversion, page 9, December 7, early editions).

HISTORY

● **16 Jul 1998**
In our Portrait of Jean Michel Jarre, Page 6, G2, July 14, we said, "and remember Napoleon never made it to Moscow". Yes he did.

● **24 Apr 2002**
In our piece about Ida Lupino, page 14, Arts, April 22, we said: "The Lupino lineage has been traced back to the Restoration, when the 'Luppinos' [sic] performed as jugglers and dancers for Charles I." That would be Charles II (Charles I did not quite make it to the Restoration).

● **5 Aug 2002**
In the obituary of Krishan Kant, India's vice-president (page 20, July 29), a grotesque misunderstanding led us to say that "Indira Gandhi sent Kant to Rajya Sabha, the 'opera house' of India's parliament". That body is, of course, the upper house of the legislature.

● **14 Nov 2002**
In our review of the film, *The Four Feathers*, page 23, November 12, we spoke of the Mahdi, as though the word described a people: "the Mahdi fall like bowling pins." Mahdi (messiah) was the title assumed by Mohammed Ahmed, the Sudanese leader who captured Khartoum in 1885 (the Mahdi's followers fall etc).

● **20 Feb 2003**
In Spanish sighs at Jeb's royal gaffe, page 13, February 18, we said that constitutional monarchy was restored in Spain by Juan Carlos II in 1975. That was Juan Carlos I.

● **15 Jul 2003**
Louis XVI was the French king who sat on the throne with his Austrian-born queen, Marie Antoinette, at the time of the revolution in 1789. It was not Louis XIV, as we wrongly stated in the subhead and text of the article, Royal revolt, Review, page 12, July 12. Louis XIV was also known as the Sun King. He died in 1715.

2 Aug 2003

Louis Blériot's flight across the English Channel was in July 1909 not 1902 as incorrectly stated in a leader, page 25, yesterday. The leader concluded by asking, "Why do all the famous crossings seem to be from England to France?" In fact, Blériot crossed from France to England.

21 Aug 2003

Several readers pointed out the mis-identification of Cardinal Richelieu with the sobriquet *éminence grise* (A place in history for British Richelieu, page 5, yesterday, front page in early editions). The name was not applied to Cardinal Richelieu himself but to his close friend, adviser and diplomatic agent, the Capuchin friar Pere Joseph (born Francois Joseph du Tremblay).

13 Sep 2003

In Restoration tragedy, page 16 of today's pre-printed Review, we suggest that Barbara Cartland was Princess Diana's grandmother. We should have said that Raine (Spencer), Cartland's daughter, was "now remembered as the stepmother of Princess Diana".

2 Dec 2003

Charles the Bold was never emperor, as we had him in a report about the Royal Academy's exhibition, Illuminating the Renaissance, page 15, November 28. He was the Duke of Burgundy, which ceased to exist as a state in the lifetime of his successor, his daughter, Mary.

3 Dec 2003

In reviewing the television programme *Matt's Old Masters*, about Rubens, page 22, G2, December 1, we referred to Philip VI of Spain. We should have said Philip IV (reigned 1621-65). There was no Philip VI; the last King Philip of Spain was Philip V (reigned 1700-46).

20 Aug 2004

In a note accompanying an article about cheese, page 8, Food, G2, August 18, we said: "For her 1858 wedding, Queen Victoria ... was presented with a giant wheel of cheddar cheese ..." Queen Victoria married Albert on February 10 1840. Her first child Victoria (Vicky) was born on November 21 that year. It was she who married in 1858.

● **11 Jan 2002**

Contrary to what we said in a column headed Return of the living dead, page 19, yesterday, *HMS Hampshire* did not sink after hitting a land mine. They are rarely found at sea.

● **14 Sep 2004**

In a short item speculating about the possible value of a coin dating from the reign of King Coenwulf (page 10, September 11), we said he ruled Mercia in the 7th century. In fact, Coenwulf reigned from 796 to 821 (the end of the 8th into the 9th centuries).

● **21 Oct 2004**

We no longer like to refer to Thomas à Becket, as we did in a leader (So hard to say sorry, page 23, October 16). We are one with medieval historians who say his name was Thomas Becket (our style guide says as much).

● **22 Nov 2004**

In explaining the spread of the use of saffron in cooking we said: "The Romans then adopted it as a spice and it was probably they who introduced it into Provence in the 11th and 12th centuries" (The spice that came in from the cold, G2, page 14, November 17). The Roman empire had gone by then, but the culinary use of saffron was spreading through the Holy Roman Empire from the Italian states.

OPEN DOOR
Unspeakable but readable

The Readers' Editor on... **unflattering views of journalism and journalists**

A column by Martin Kettle in which he extolled the virtues of the American writer Henry David Thoreau as revealed in his *Walden*, reminded me of something Thoreau had to say in that book on the subject of newspapers: "Why should our life be in any respect provincial? If we will read newspapers, why not skip the gossip of Boston and take the best newspaper in the world at once? – not be sucking the pap of 'neutral family' papers ..."

This quotation made a great impression on me more than 30 years ago, partly because I had already been working for about 15 years in journalism in what were sometimes called the provinces (the company for which I worked was at one time called Provincial Newspapers). Thoreau's was one of the first of many comments on journalism, or on journalists, that I noted down as worth remembering.

It was also one of the few that could be held to say something positive about journalism, even allowing for Thoreau's implication that the "family" newspaper with its bland regurgitated version of things was not worth reading at all. At least it held up the possibility of something more challenging and useful if only we were to define it and then demand it.

Most of the comments that struck me had nothing very good to say about the business of journalism. That may be because I gleaned most of them from "literary" sources, so in that sense they were gathered accidentally from my normal reading.

About the time that this habit was taking root Weidenfeld and Nicolson published John *Gross's The Rise and Fall of the Man of Letters* (1969). Gross declared: "Journalism is a career; literature is, or ought to be, a vocation." Gross continued, "Few major 19th-century writers would have gone quite as far as John Ruskin, who dismissed the entire output of Fleet Street as 'so many square leagues of dirtily printed falsehood', but most of them viewed the growth of the press as a very mixed blessing indeed. It gave them a powerful new platform, and at the same time drowned out what they were trying to say with triviality and claptrap."

Journalism, the message seemed to be, was something real writers only deigned or stooped to do. The message did not seem to vary much according to time or place. A recent addition is from Henry James's *The Portrait of a Lady*, in which journalism is ironically fused or confused with literature: "Mrs Varian's acquaintance with literature was confined to *The New York Interviewer*; as she very justly said, after you had read the *Interviewer* you had lost all faith in culture." There is a particularly memorable line when Isabel, the heroine, accuses her friend, Henrietta Stackpole, the journalist from the *Interviewer*, of having no sense of privacy. "'You do me great injustice,' said Miss Stackpole with dignity. 'I've never written a word about myself!'"

Among the early quotations I jotted down were two from Karl Kraus, the Austrian satirist (1874-1936): "Journalists write because they have nothing to say, and they have something to say because they write," and "A journalist is stimulated by a deadline: he writes worse when he has time." Both of those come from WH Auden's commonplace book *A Certain World* (Faber, 1970), and spurred me on to find and read more KK, rewarding me with: "No ideas and the ability to express them – that's a journalist." (*No Compromise*, selected writings of Karl Kraus, Frederick Ungar, New York, 1977).

Chekhov, expressing shame over some of his early newspaper pieces, wrote: "The word 'newspaper-writer' means, at very least, a scoundrel. I'm one of them, I work with them, I shake hands with them, I'm even told that I've begun to look like one ... But, I shan't die as one." (from VS Pritchett: *Chekhov, A Spirit Set Free*, Random House, 1988).

I could go on (on and on, as a matter of fact). It is not all one-sided. We overlook great figures such as William Hazlitt and Leigh Hunt. The latter, writing against slavery, said: "The history of opinion tells us never to despair of effecting the ruin of prejudice."

And Auden himself, in *A Certain World*, had particular praise for the journalist who digs out "cases of injustice, cruelty, corruption, which the authorities would like to keep hidden, and which even the average reader would prefer not to be compelled to think about". Contributions and references are welcome.

28 Aug 2004

HOMOPHONES

17 Mar 1998

In a report on page 7, yesterday, headed Chauvinist bosses are sex pests, we said: "Among the more outrageous demands of employers was a request for details of one secretary's menstrual cycle so that her boss could 'give her a wide birth'." We should have said berth.

9 Jul 1998

We persist in peddling peddle instead of pedal. On page 9, G2, July 6, ignoring earlier corrections, we referred to peddle pushers in an article, Soft shoe shuffle. The things on each side of a bicycle are pedals.

10 August 1998

A reference to "mushy pees" appeared in an article about Northumberland Place, London W2, yesterday (page7, G2): mushy peas was what the columnist had in mind.

3 Sep 1998

The tenderhooks that someone was on in Ballybunion in anticipation of President Clinton's visit, Page 7, September 1, should have been tenterhooks.

7 Nov 1998

In last week's Saturday Review, page 4, October 31, in Guru in a gas mask, we said that someone had just "hawked" himself to the eyebrows ... We meant to say hocked.

26 Nov 1998

In a report, Targets for devil worship, Page 3, November 24, we said that the name of a satanic goddess "had been daubed on the wall and a fire lit in the knave".

1 Dec 1998

A column in the comment section (page 16, yesterday) contained the sentence: "Marianne herself, bearing one breast as she strode across the barricades, had been kept from me."

● **3 Mar 1999**

A quoted remark on Page 1, March 1, "We have to stop this project before the British government is party to fermenting war in the Middle East ..."

● **11 Jan 2000**

Homophone corner, from a short profile of Monica Mason, of the Royal Ballet, page 14, January 8. The role in *Giselle* is not Queen of the Willies. It is Queen of the Wilis. A wili is the ghost of a girl who died betrayed by her lover.

● **17 Mar 2000**

From Poseur index, a feature on page 4, Space, a supplement with some editions, yesterday, "So what if I live in an ex-council flat in central London with a dirty old lift but a rather fine rubbish shoot ..."

● **27 May 2000**

From page 2 of G2, yesterday, "... plants on their own are one thing but when you put them together they compliment each other".

● **7 Jun 2001**

Another (near) homophone, from advice for safety in the sun, Education, page 68, June 5: "Where a wide-brimmed hat." Where indeed.

● **5 Mar 2002**

In Country Diary, page 16, March 1, we said that the horses used by Northumbria Police were chosen "for temperament and confirmation". That should have said "conformation".

● **24 Jun 2002**

In an article about *Abigail's Party*, pages 10 and 11, G2, June 19, we quoted Mike Leigh, the director, saying Alison Steadman's character, Beverly, was "completely subdued by received notions of how we should behave and what we should have". Mike Leigh points out that her character in fact is anything but subdued. What he actually said (in a telephone interview) was that Beverly was "imbued with received notions ..." etc.

● **12 Jul 2002**

"The audience was encouraged to wander over the stage and activate hidden censors," said our story on a coming production of *The Embalmers*, page 14, G2, July 10. Sensors!

● **11 Sep 2002**

In our notes about the BBC2 programme, *The Ship*, page 75, the Guide, September 7, we said that the 2,000-mile ocean voyage was made "even saltier by the fact that David, John and Jay only possess woefully inaccurate 18th century charts and a sexton".

21 Sep 2002

From page 5, yesterday, "I suppose I'm a bit of a loose canon." Not at all.

15 Nov 2002

From a report on page 4, November 11, "After 22 years of service he earns £29,000 a year plus £3,000 extra for London waiting." (Corrected for later editions).

8 Feb 2003

From Country Diary, page 16, G2, yesterday: "We did not waste many of the richly yoked eggs that free range hens gave us ..."

From Etcetera, page 19, G2, yesterday: "Any cow that can survive a duel carriageway ... has got to be pretty damn lucky ..."

4 Mar 2003

From a column, page 16, February 26: "There were few 'Here, heres!' from the Labour benches ..."

8 Dec 2003

From a column, page 27, December 5: "This week [Tony Blair] and Charles Clarke drove themselves wrecklessly into a dead end ..."

13 Dec 2003

From page 16 of yesterday's Friday Review: "Dracula's sexual potency is given its full reign."

14 Jan 2004

From The real Howard Dean, page 6, G2, January 12: "In New Hampshire, the first major primary, the poles uniformly suggest that Dean is running way ahead of his nearest rival, Senator John Kerry ..."

28 Apr 2004

From TV review, page 22, G2, yesterday: "There could be a timpani roll, or a crash of symbols as they're ejected from the front door."

6 May 2004

On rowing: "If you were going to make an argument for something it would be the single skull or the eight" (from page 20, Sport, May 3).

12 May 2004

From an obituary, page 25, May 8: "Before he could read, he was pouring over pictures in *Country Life*."

15 Jun 2004

"His grotesque facial tick might frighten the boys" (The prize quiz, G2, page 23, June 9).

⬤ 14 Jul 2004

In a report, Pilot to visit bombed church, page 8, July 12, we said (early editions only) that an unexploded bomb "came to rest in the knave" (corrected for later editions).

⬤ 27 Nov 2004

"I had spent several days alone in the house going through cupboards full of old photographs and, stealing myself, had binned thousands of snaps" (Heartbreak house, page 15, G2, November 24).

⬤ 13 Jan 2005

From page 13, Travel, January 8: "In the estimable Blueberry's Tea Room we eat minced beef and leak pudding ..."

⬤ 14 Jan 2005

"Panjabi plays a westernised young Asian woman whose father has made her marry her Pakistani goatheard cousin" (from page 16, G2, yesterday).

⬤ 27 Jan 2005

From a sports report, page 28, January 25: "Then, like a weather front sweeping in off the Great Austrian Bite, all changed."

OPEN DOOR
An inconclusive game of marbles

The Readers' Editor on... **the vague origins of a popular pejorative expression**

A week ago the Guardian carried a review by the former chairman of the BBC Gavyn Davies, of the memoirs of the former director general of the corporation Greg Dyke. In it he said: "Greg says that, in pursuing an illegitimate complaint, [Alastair] Campbell behaved like 'a deranged, vindictive bastard', on the verge of losing a full set of marbles."

The reference to marbles caught a reader's attention. "What is the derivation of this phrase? Why should losing one's mind be associated with marbles?" In this particular case, the reviewer offered what amounted to an explanation and qualification of its meaning: "In my view, Campbell has many admirable qualities, but was undoubtedly going through a bad patch which made life for the rest of us (the prime minister, for example) almost impossible." The context is the angry turmoil attending the Gilligan affair.

It is not a phrase that crops up in the Guardian very often and it is usually used with a non-serious or jocular intent. One of its fairly rare appearances – almost five years ago – was in a headline that read: "Why losing one's marbles isn't all bad." The story was about the Elgin marbles.

The reader's query nicely coincided with the arrival on my desk of a new book by Nigel Rees, *A Word in Your Shell-like: 6,000 Curious and Everyday Phrases Explained* (Collins) – a treasury of stimulating excursions and digressions in the English language. Rees actually explores but dismisses the association of the phrase with the Elgin marbles. "At the popular level," he says, "most people believe the phrase derives from a joke. When Lord Elgin brought back his famous marbles from the Parthenon and they ended up in the British Museum in 1816, the Greeks were hopping mad (and, indeed, remain so). But, with all due respect and however entertaining, this is not an origin to be taken seriously."

According to Rees, "almost everyone" agrees that the expression is American in origin and he notes that the *Oxford English Dictionary* finds it first recorded in the journal *American Speech* in 1927. In fact, the OED (Supplement, 1976) provides the actual example from *American Speech*: "There goes a man who doesn't have all his marbles."

Rees explores the possible association of the phrase with the French *meubles*, "furniture, movables" (which the *OED* describes as a false translation), and asks, "Could one imagine 'to lose one's marbles' coming from the idea of losing one's 'mind furniture'?" He quotes in support two sayings that use furniture as an indicator of mental well-being or the lack of it. One is from a correspondent in Cheshire who notes there the expression, "He's got all his chairs at home" and one from a correspondent in Yorkshire who wrote, "If someone is a bit lacking in the head, we say that they haven't got all their furniture at home." Hence, Rees suggests, "a home without furniture is empty, so 'lost one's marbles' = empty-headed, no longer at home, no longer 'there'."

One of the examples that he calls in support actually seems to me to argue an altogether more direct and plausible origin. It comes from a publication of the English Dialect Society (*West Cornwall Words*) in 1880: "Those that have marbles may play, but those that have none must look on." Rees says: "Surely this admirably conveys the misfortune of those who are without the necessary wherewithal to participate in the game of life?"

So it does but, unless I am losing my marbles, it is simply making an illustrative reference to the game of marbles (for a history see www.marblemuseum.org). The *OED* cites references to the game from English sources from around the beginning of the 18th century. The *OED Supplement*, by the way, equates the word with mental faculties, brains, or common sense. Although it doesn't make the direct connection between the game and the use of the word according to that definition, none of the examples it quotes seem incompatible with the idea. To give a couple of them: "Do men who have got all their marbles go swimming in lakes with their clothes on?" (PG Wodehouse's *Cocktail Time*, 1958); "You lost your goddam' marbles? You gone completely crazy, you nutty slob?" (John Wainwright's *The Take-Over Men*, 1969). Certainly not the sort of language we like to see in the Guardian.

Forgive me for digressing, but as I found while browsing in Nigel Rees's book, one thing leads to another and it's a short step from the sublime to the ridiculous (Rees, page 639).

2 Oct 2004

SCIENCE

16 Nov 1998

Faradisation was a form of electro-therapy and not – as we said in a television review, page 19, G2, November 9 – "better known as electrocution". Just to be clear about it, electrocution is death by electric shock.

16 Mar 1999

In an article on page 3, Saturday Review, March 13, headed Let us into the tower of knowledge, we said "biology is rarely more complicated than Morse code". What the biologist who wrote the piece actually said was "biology is rarely more complicated than Morse" – meaning the television series of that name, noted for the subtlety of its plots.

1 Jun 1999

Salicylic acid, page 29, May 26, Drug find robs Britain of Olympic place, may be found in willow bark, rather than willow herb (*Britannica*).

26 Feb 2000

In a piece about BBC weather presenters, Turned out beautiful again, page 5, G2, February 22, the writer suggested that one of them, David Braine, at 37 was "no spring solstice any more". He never was. There is no spring solstice. There is a summer solstice, a winter solstice, an autumn equinox and a spring equinox.

5 Aug 2000

In a report relating how dangerous bacteria had mistakenly been sent to the curtain department of Debenhams in Plymouth, page 9, yesterday, we referred to the intended recipient, CAMR, the centre for applied microbiology and research at Porton Down. However, midway through the story, we said the phials had been collected from the store within 24 hours by a representative of CAMRA. The latter is the Campaign for Real Ale, which had nothing to do with it.

15 Dec 2000

In a column, page 7, Society, December 13, we said: "In the words of Lord Rothschild, boss of the former think tank, their role is to produce the grit which creates the oyster." More valuably, the grit creates the pearl (in some oysters).

22 Feb 2001

In an article on page 2 of the Science section, February 15, we said: "Out of more than 4,000 types of amphibians we have reproductive information on a handful of species. The variation is enormous: blind snakes ... sea snakes ... crocodiles ..." None of these is an amphibian. They are all reptiles. London Zoo says so.

11 Dec 2002

An error was introduced into our Friday Review cover story about George Formby, December 6. We said, "Formby remains the only British person to be awarded the Order of Lenin." In fact, the George Formby Society has found no trace of such an award being made.

7 Mar 2001

In a letter in Weekend, page 5, March 3, we had the writer say "the average glass of milk contains 112,899,408-plus cells". That should have been pus cells.

31 May 2001

Our At home roundup, page 3, the Editor, May 26, included a reference to a "silicon-enhanced model". On page 6 of the same issue of the Editor, we said the woman in question was "famous for having more silicon than ... Silicon Valley". What she perhaps has is silicone, the compound commonly used for breast implants. Silicon Valley is correct.

29 Aug 2001

In our leader on the funding of science research, Who pays the piper? page 15, August 27, we said that the aorta carries blood to the heart when in fact it carries blood away from the heart.

5 Jul 2002

In a report, Helicopters rescue polar researchers trapped in ice, page 2, July 2, we said (in early editions only), 90 people were ferried across ice floes "as the hours of daylight grew shorter and shorter in the past week". In fact, since the events took place in the Antarctic, the hours of daylight would have been slowly growing (while shortening in the northern hemisphere).

● **15 Aug 2002**

Creatures in the group that embraces insects and arachnids are arthropods and not arthopods as we had it in our report, Fatal fever that lurks in the swamps, page 3, August 13.

● **19 Aug 2002**

Bacteria are plural but we are not always prepared to admit it. In a brief report, Swiss cheese sees off acne, page 9, Online, August 8, we said, "the acne bacteria was controlled ..." In an item correctly headed Bacteria close swimming pool, page 6, August 15, we lapsed into the singular in the text, with "the bacteria that can cause legionnaire's [sic] disease was found in a water tank". Legionnaires' disease is caused by the bacterium *Legionella pneumophila*.

● **25 Sep 2002**

In a leader, When the earth moved, page 21, yesterday, we said there were "five miles of earth" above the "epicentre" of the Dudley earthquake. We should have said above the "focus". The epicentre of an earthquake is the point on the earth's surface directly above the "focus" – the point below the ground at which the earthquake occurs.

● **6 Dec 2002**

In an article, Britain and US step up bombing in Iraq, page 17, December 4, we said, "British military sources say they are concerned in particular about Iraq's carbon-fibre communications network ..." We meant to say fibre-optic, not carbon-fibre.

● **19 Mar 2003**

In an article about the "new disease", severe acute respiratory syndrome, page 8, Health G2, yesterday, we said one of the symptoms was a high fever of 38.6F. We meant 38.6C.

● **13 Aug 2003**

Australopithecus is not the shared ancestor of humans and chimps, as we suggested in a caption on page 10 of Life, August 7. Early humans and chimpanzees diverged millions of years before Australopithecus existed.

● **11 Feb 2004**

In our review of the El Greco exhibition, pages 12 and 13, G2, yesterday, we said the artist "bore a son". Women bear the children.

15 Jul 2004

The lion mare jellyfish referred to in a report, Sting in the tale for careless swimmers, page 10, July 9, is the lion's mane jellyfish.

24 Jul 2004

Weatherwatch reported a typically hot day in Dakar at 29C/84F with, incredibly, snow (page 28, July 22). The agency which supplies us with the data explains: "The weather elements observed from each station across the world are sent in a coded message. The observer at Dakar on the 21st reported current weather type 22 which is recent snow. He or she meant to report 2 (sunny)."

28 Jul 2004

The dirigible *Hindenburg* was not powered by hydrogen, as we said in our report, Boost for hydrogen buses, page 20, July 26. It was lifted by 7 million cubic feet of hydrogen but propelled by four 16-cylinder diesel engines.

25 Aug 2004

In early editions of our leader, Tears for Paula [Radcliffe], page 15, August 23, we referred to her ordeal in "brutal temperatures" well above 30 degrees C (100 degrees F). In fact 30C is about 86F. Later editions had "35C (95F)".

12 Jan 2005

A report, Reed cutters fight back as imports from east cut into a dying craft, page 6, January 4, referred to "stinking methane produced by the reed". Methane does not stink (it is odourless), and it does not come from the reed (it is produced by anaerobic microbes in the mud).

OPEN DOOR
Showcasing Guardian English

The Readers' Editor on... **words that strike a jarring note**

It would be possible to devote this column every week, instead of just occasionally, to readers' comments and queries about the Guardian's use of English. The concern for style and correct usage, a reader tells me, is one of the things (or should it be two of the things?) that he particularly likes about the paper. But ... What had irritated him on this occasion was a headline that read, "Alistair Cooke's final collection [of his *Letters from America*] showcases his incisive and prescient commentary on the country he loved".

"The use of 'showcase' as a verb has frequently been used in your pages and the use of it in this particular context grates on the eye and ear because Alistair Cooke himself never failed to use the English language with precision in everything he said or wrote," explained the reader, who went on to suggest that "the simple verbs which could be used are: display, exhibit, reveal, demonstrate, or even simply show".

He then offers a cautionary quote from George Orwell's description of Newspeak: "Any word in the language could be used as either verb, noun, adjective or adverb ... By such methods it was found possible to bring about an enormous diminution of vocabulary."

This reader lives in Wirral, a point I mention, not to suggest that readers there are more pernickety about these things, but to make the point that he would have received an early edition. "Showcases" clearly grated on other ears because for later editions the heading became: "Alistair Cooke's final collection continues his incisive and prescient commentary on the country he loved". It was changed, presumably, not because it was wrong but because it was dissonant. We do not like it and we assume that Alistair Cooke did not like it either.

As a verb, it is a relative newcomer to our vocabulary. It does not appear in the first edition of the *Oxford English Dictionary*, either as a word in its own right or in relation to "show", the entries for which occupy several pages. It does, however, appear in the supplement of 1986, where its origin is given as the United States, and its meaning as: "To place in, or as in a showcase (chiefly figurative)." Interestingly, the first quoted example of its use, in 1945, by HL Mencken, was pointing to an earlier existence. Writing in a supplement to *American Language*, and referring to the showbusiness magazine *Variety*, Mencken said, "A few of its characteristic inventions will suffice: to ash-can, to angel, to showcase [etc]."